Experience Joy

More Than Being Happy or Joyful,
Learn How Your Personal Resonance
Can Create the Life Changing Experience of Joy!

Experience Joy

Joshua R. Henriot

Experience Joy ©2021 Joshua R Henriot; All Rights Reserved.

No part of this publication may be reproduced, distributed or transmitted in any form or by any means without the prior written permission of the publisher, except in the case of brief quotations embodied in critical reviews and certain other noncommercial uses permitted by copywrite law.

Although the author and publisher have made every effort to ensure that the information in this book was accurate at press time, the author and publisher do not assume and hereby disclaim any liability to any party for any loss, damage, or disruption caused by errors and omissions, whether such errors or omissions result from negligence, accident, or any other cause.

Obeying all applicable laws and regulations, including international, federal, state and local governing professional licensing, business practices, advertising, and all other aspects of doing business in the US, Canada or any other jurisdiction is the sole responsibility of the reader and consumer.

Neither the author nor the publisher assumes any responsibility or liability on behalf of the consumer or reader of this material. Any perceived slight of any individual or organization is entirely unintentional.
The resources in this book are provided for informational and recreational purposes only and should not be used to replace the specialized training and professional judgement of health care professionals.

Neither the author nor the publisher can be held responsible for the use of the information within this book. Always consult trained professionals before making any decisions regarding medical, mental, emotional, or spiritual treatment or changes for yourself or your family.

ISBN: 979-8-9850099-0-3 (Hardback)
ISBN: 979-8-9850099-2-7 (Paperback)
ISBN: 979-8-9850099-1-0 (Ebook)

FORWARD

Every once in a while, I will have the privilege to engage in a project that is so life-giving and transformative, I come away from it forever changed. Such has been the case with the book you now hold in your hands, which I had the privilege of editing.

With keen insights and imaginative contextualization, Joshua employs elements of game theory to everyday life, calling each of us to be open to an encounter with Joy. Far from being an inspirational book about Joy, we are treated to a banquet of sensory, sensational, and scientific delicacies that delight the reader. I stepped away from each chapter wanting to "level up" my life in greater capacity and apprehension of the possibilities of engaging Joy.

In this very personal account, Joshua Henriot cleverly calls each of his readers to glimpse the possibilities that linger just beyond the veil of an experience … an Experience with Joy.

In early computer games, you were provided with a handy tool that gave you access to the field of play within the game: the appropriately named "Joystick". In the game of life, the volume you have before you is a "next level" Joy Stick. Settle into your comfortable gaming chair, pick up this book, and press start. You may just be embarking on an epic adventure as you Experience Joy!

Steve Hampton
Everett, Washington

Table of Contents

Preface — 1

PART 1 — 9
The Experience of Joy -v- The State of Being Joyful

Chapter 1 — 13
What is The Experience of Joy?

Chapter 2 — 17
What is Being Joyful?

PART 2 — 21
The "Experience of Joy" Game

Chapter 3 — 25
The Rules, Objective, Gameboard, Players,
Game Pieces, Artifacts, Movement/Play

Chapter 4 — 37
Power ups, Level Ups, and Bonuses

PART 3   47
Internal Coherence

Chapter 5   51
The Mind – Brain Resonance

Chapter 6   57
The Heart – Soul Resonance

Chapter 7   63
The Gut – Instinct Resonance

Chapter 8   67
The Genes – Spirit Resonance

PART 4   75
External Coherence

Chapter 9   79
Resonate with your gameboard.

Chapter 10   83
Resonate with your inputs and senses.

Chapter 11   93
Resonate with your Feelings and Emotions – Reactions to External Stimuli

Chapter 12   99
Resonate with another, a purpose, a group, or community

PART 5   105
Dissonance and Discordance

Chapter 13   109
The Obstacles

Closing   115
Bibliography   119
Dictionary   125
Further Readings: 143

Preface

I felt awkward being joyful all the time. Rarely did I meet anyone else who was joyful, or even happy; and walking around in a state of bliss for no apparent reason started to make me feel out of place. There seemed to be discordance everywhere, and I just didn't relate.

Then it happened. Driving home from work – while driving – I had an "Experience of Joy." January 26th, 2021. Imprinted – date, time, what I was doing, where I was. The entire Experience, like other memories I've had for a long time, cherished, embellished, comfortable. This experience changed me foundationally. It connected me to something larger, in a way I never knew existed, and epigenetically altered my DNA. Something got turned on, or turned off, or whatever. I resonated, in a vibrational state without tremors - a supernatural tuning.

I was impacted and changed enough to write a book about it. What happened, what it was, what it felt like, and how I was able to repeat the experience. The state of being joyful can be very intense, Experiencing Joy is life changing.

This book is for everyone who wants to know what the Experience of Joy is, what it feels like, what it does for you, and how to prepare for it, intentionally. Space travel is to riding your bike like the Experience of Joy is to being joyful. The Experience of Joy is available to everyone to experience and hold in your memories, and to meditate on when thinking about the next stage of your life. This is not about the state of being joyful. It is about Experiencing Joy.

Being joyful is a choice, the Experience of Joy is spontaneous and life changing. It is a traumatic change in emotional intelligence, intellectual awareness, and relational resonance within. Sometimes called a mystical experience and I can understand why, but it isn't. It is a resonance among the physical and non-physical self, the corporal and the ethereal.

Joe Dispenza teaches that the desire or forethought for the next stage in your life, paired with the emotion of achieving, or being in possession, of your desire activates attraction in the universe and has proven results. Experiencing Joy is a personal resonance of your desires with your emotional awareness. By learning how to Experience Joy you can pair an intense emotional awareness of resonance with conscious desire and positively impact your life.

I've learned that coherence within or amongst tribes-groups-communities have resonated together and won championships, climbed mountains, run governments, and created celebrated events by congealing together around a common cause. Hajj, Burning Man, protests, wars. Not for the faint of heart and effort, but a cohesive continuation of intentional resonance and motivations. A new motivation for Spirit Week at school, swag at work, and the earnest desire of leaders to inspire everywhere. Vibrational resonance increases with additional coherence. An individual is powerful, two is stronger than one, and get a group in the same wavelength and watch miracles happen.

It is by resonating within that we Experience Joy, and the Experience of Joy resonates with us and increases our personal power. Resonance with ourselves, with our family, with our communities (local, expanded, global) gives us a resonance that when paired with the right environment and intentional inputs creates a sense of intense bliss, contentment, and an internal resonance that prepares us to Experience Joy.

The first step is to resonate with yourself, and while most people want to shortcut to the end results, if you are internally discordant your results will be dissonant, and that may explain some things in life. Let's look at our priorities in life and the time we spend on those priorities as an example.

COHERENCE		DISCORDANCE	
Priorities	Time	Priorities	Time
1	1	1	4
2	2	2	2
3	3	3	6
4	4	4	1
5	5	5	7
6	6	6	3
7	7	7	5

This diagram shows the difference in priorities and time spent on those priorities, and you can see what discordance looks like in life

When the time in our lives matches our priorities in life then it could be said we are in coherence. When your internally important aspects – your personal priorities – do not match the time spent on activities then you can easily see the chaos, stress, and discordance that can result.

If you don't love yourself, how do you think loving someone else will work out? It all starts at home, alone, in the dark, silent hours where we have nothing but ourselves and our thoughts. In the gap between actions and thoughts. No devices, no visual, auditory, or other sensory inputs. What are you? Who are you? When are you? How are you? Where are you? This internal evaluation is where the Experience of Joy starts as you begin to understand your personal resonance. This book is not about finding yourself; it is about the resonance within yourself that opens your opportunity to Experience Joy.

What's your favorite color, food, activity, subject in school, hobby, etc. Have you ever asked yourself? Have you ever investigated and tried to understand what others have explained about when you were born? Were you born in the Year of the Lion? Is your success number 7? What's your zodiac sign? For my entire life, blue was my favorite color, and when I wore the right color, it made my eyes look even brighter and I got thousands of comments throughout my life about my blue eyes. I recently found out that blue is my health color, and red is my success color. I have only had moderate success in my life, but I've had excellent health and continue very healthy to this day. I still love blue! Red is my success color, and just today I found my two blue t-shirts at the bottom of my t-shirts. I'm wearing red.

During the afterglow of my initial Experience of Joy I had the vision of preparing for the Experience of Joy being a game, where you gain specific knowledge, items, and abilities to level up to increased levels, increasing your personal power and vibrational resonance. Just like in games where you gain armor, weapons, skills, potions to win the next level you can prepare yourself for the Experience of Joy by gaining resonance power ups. This was a dream I had, one of those vivid reality TV shows of the mind where each cognizant realization of resonance made me more powerful but only to myself. It was a challenge for me to achieve independent of anything or anyone else, although everything and everyone was there. As I learned every level I went to the next level and had to learn those skills, acquire and then understand those artifacts, etc. I was almost to the highest level of the game when I woke up, feeling thwarted of that final achievement by my circadian rhythm. I was left with an intense desire to achieve more, but instinctively knew that there was no known top level.

In this game we accomplish tasks to power up to the next level, just like any other game. We start with a power level of 0.1, and our first task is to learn how to resonate with ourselves, progressing through this level with specific things to do and realize about ourselves, gaining power and resonance, until resonance with self is achieved, a single unit, the power level of 1.0. From there we'll learn how to multiply our power through resonance with others, friends, family, lovers, groups, cohorts, tribes, communities, even globally.

Here is the first challenge – you never stop learning about yourself, and we change as we acquire experience. (There is a time factor in getting experience sometimes called aging.)

You may not know how much you like sailing, for example, until you have the experience of gliding effortlessly and silently across the water with grace and power – it's intoxicating for some and sickening for others. Substitute music, food, or any other activity for sailing. Gaining this knowledge about yourself in the present moment, your present moment, is part of your powering up to a more advanced level. Think of needing to gather items – experiences, artifacts, knowledge - to complete your level and then moving up. Having friends, appreciating family, knowing your current style (we know that changes), and being conscious of your current state of health – mind, body, emotional, and relational - could be items to gather for you to move from .1 to .2, for example. As we learn more about ourselves, we will be able to stay coherent with ourselves because although our lives change as we gain experience (our styles, foods, family all change) we have already learned how to resonate with ourselves.

There are a bajillion resources to understand getting to know yourself. This step is not about self-awareness, but about *connecting*. There are questionnaires online, lots of books, and I mean LOTS on all aspects of getting to know yourself spiritually, emotionally, and physically. When it comes to this step, nothing else will resonate, nothing else will jive, nothing else gives us the power to level up in life until we get this part right. And there are two parts to us that we will need to learn how to connect: the corporal, or physical parts, and the ethereal, or non-physical parts. Incorporating this self-knowledge could be referred to as embodied cognition, colloquially called self-recognition.

The embodied cognition of our contemplated physical presence is only knowledge. Connect with the vibrational resonance of our physical presence with our conscious embodied cognition – who we are with what we are – tunes our internal symphony. Like a symphony tuning, all those disparate/discordant sounds from 100's of instruments getting ready to play; once they're warmed up and in tune the conductor taps their baton and there is a gap, a silent moment before the symphonic experience begins. In this moment, this gap, everything has been prepared, readied, and simply waits. There is anticipation, yearning, and magic in this gap, this quiet stillness, poised for symphonic resonance, or an Experience of Joy!

Let's learn the game, the magic in the gap, and Experience Joy!

PART 1

The Experience of Joy -v-
The State of Being Joyful

Opening

There is a difference between feeling joyful and the Experience of Joy. The feeling of joy is an emotion that you feel, and the Experience of Joy is an actual physical and spiritual event, activity, something that happens.

As an emotion the feeling of joy exists on a spectrum like many other things including sexuality, gender identity, skin color, race, love, sadness, anger, temperature, and states of disagreement. It's all on a spectrum from the weakest to the strongest, and while I've walked around feeling joyful for a long time, I've only had a few Experiences of Joy. The intensity of any one Experience of Joy greater than the sum of all the years of feeling joyful.

As an emotion, feeling joyful is something I can choose to do, while an Experience of Joy is something that happens in or to me. I can't go get an Experience of Joy like I can walk down to the corner coffee shop and get a Latte. Lots of emotions are choices, like which coffee shop to choose, although some emotions may be reactionary to circumstances in our lives, we've actuality chosen and all but preprogrammed how we'll feel when things happen. And if we don't comply with our own or the community's expected emotional response, we are anomalous. This is a key concept.

To be outside the expectation is to be anomalous, and it is the anomalous that experience different things, outside expectations. To be happy in traffic or watching the news, joyful in failure, excited being thwarted. These contradictory reactions are simply anomalous to expectation, and produce change; sometimes drastic change, sometime incremental change, but change absolutely. And change happens only when non-compliant with expectations. We are talking about Experiencing Joy. It is not normal, and it might require change. It will absolutely require accepting new knowledge.

PART 1

Chapter 1

What is The Experience of Joy?

The Experience of Joy is not a fleeting moment of feeling to be forgotten as soon as it leaves. The Experience of Joy impacts and changes us – traumatizes us – in an indelible way, as if tattooed with the experience like a Moana® tattoo. Our lives – body and soul – are changed by the Experience of Joy with an energy signal/vibration/resonance that adds to our personal resonance. We all have a personal persona, character, personality, attitude, and feeling of power at some level. Every Experience of joy we have permanently adds to our personal power level, increases our coherence, and this book explains how to Experience Joy and add to your personal power level!

Joy is a high-level emotion that is complex by nature. I have never met anyone who's emotions were simple, single dimensional experiences. Emotion's intensity varies from the least intense to incredibly severe, on a spectrum, from frustrated to angry, like to love, happy to joyful, and sad to depressed, etc. Joy is near the high end of the highest spectrum, and once you get there, you will never lose the reward for getting there. You never lose the tattoo, full color, deep clean blacks, and expertly shaded. The Experience of Joy is an *indelible experience*.

The Experience of Joy is different from being joyful. Many people talk about feeling joyful or being joyful, but I've never heard another talk about an Experience of Joy. There isn't a pill, a set of steps, simply some knowledge about joy or even an experience to have to suddenly be able to Experience Joy. The Experience of Joy is not the cause or result of something specific, like an episode of a sitcom. The Experience of Joy is a combination of physical, non-physical, and emotional coherence, the vibration of self in concert. The Joy Experience is a full-body explosion of intense resonance, an intense expansion of conscious realization. In Joy we have the ethereal feeling of being bigger than a Thanksgiving Day Parade balloon. We cannot get to this expansive awareness by walking into it, but we can prepare ourselves to Experience Joy. We can tune ourselves as instruments, ready to play the music of our lives, ready to Experience Joy.

In a symphony, musical vibrations are produced by musicians, musical instruments, and instructions. There is the physical body, the musicians, instruments, and instructions, and they produce the physical/non-physical sound of the music. We receive, willingly, the sound input, but we can't touch or see the sound, although we may feel it. When we hear the music, our brain processes the input, and our heart feels the sound with complimentary vibrations. We do not need to be the musician with all that skill and training to sense the vibrations that create the melody we feel, but the more we understand about how vibrations vibrate within us the more in tune our life experience will be. Where do you hear music? In your head? Your heart? Rumbling in your torso, your gut? Have you ever *experienced* music as well as heard or felt it? We have capacity to hear music, and by learning a little bit more about listening, feeling the vibrations, we will expand our conscious comprehension of the concert. We will experience the music, and Experiencing Joy is similar. You can be in a joyful state, like hearing the music, and then you can transcend and Experience Joy like you can experience music.

Hearing the music is not simply a matter of attending the concert. Anyone ever been at an event where someone else, perhaps yourself, was not happy about it? Not 'in tune' with the event? That unhappy person is discordant, vibrating out of tune, out of coherence with the group, the event. Contrast that with an experience with friends where everyone is excited, looking forward to the event, feeding off and contributing to the others experience. We all experience similar things and can learn to vibrate in coherence – resonate - with that experience. It is a skill that can be intentionally developed, practiced, and employed to improve our personal power.

When I started this journey to write about my Experience of Joy, I had a vision about it being a game, where we level up – power up - in each section. Each step within a level is interchangeable, but in general the levels must be completed in order. I haven't seen anyone able to Experience Joy without completing level one – connecting with yourself. A disconnection with yourself is the most discordant state to be in.

The object of the game is NOT to be more joyful, happy, free, giddy, smiley faced and syrupy sweet. The object of the game is to have an Experience of Joy. The Experience of Joy is overwhelming, completely consuming, an expansion of self in a ballooning of all senses encompassing the higher vibrational states of Love, Joy, Peace, and Enlightenment. It can last for a few moments or longer. Each instance of Joy you Experience traumatizes you forward with a sudden enhancement of life. An instance of Experiencing Joy moves you to a higher level in life.

Connect with the Experience of Joy community at **www.thejoyguy.com** and share your Experience!

PART 1

Chapter 2

What is Being Joyful?

The Experience of Joy is different from *being joyful* in that Joy is an experience and *being joyful* is a *state* of *being*. We can go through life full time or part time in a state of being joyful and never really experience the life changing Experience of Joy. We talk of many things as being joyful; what we see, feel, touch, or experience. These are all physical pleasures from inputs we receive that are an aspect of experiencing joy but not the Experience of Joy itself. The Experience of Joy is connecting, it blends you into something more – within you and outside of you. When we have physical pleasures, they may be joyful, intense, but it may or may not connect us. In the moments of joyful experiences that connect with us, resonate with us, we approach the Experience of Joy. When the physical joyful experience entraps us in connecting resonance, we Experience Joy.

My experiences started in my gut and grew through increased corporal and ethereal coherent vibration in the sacral and lumbar plexus regions of the parasympathetic nerve pathway with an intense resonance. In other words, from the bottom up. The resonance grew, startlingly quickly, suddenly, and once out of my gut my heart and brain began to resonate in coherence, and the alertness and awareness of being greater than physical connected me to the universe, the zero-point field, the holy spirit, Gaia, myself. As overwhelming as it was, it was fulfilling – not too much or too little, and as soon as it dimmed, I yearned for it again. Fortunately, I was close to home, and after parking I was left dumbfounded, traumatized, trying to make sense of an experience I had never had before. Everything seemed different. I felt as though I knew more, could see more, understood more, and resonated with a little higher vibration, to myself, to my wife, to the world. The after effect lasted for more than a week, almost 10 full days. In a matter of a few moments my perception, understanding, and life had changed.

The afterglow of Experiencing Joy is the state of being joyful. The afterglow of an Experience of Joy is also the preceding game play for Experiencing Joy! By investing in learning how we can resonate, and be coherent with what connects with us and allowing that resonance to vibrate within us, we establish within ourselves an internal symphony, ready to play, ready to Experience Joy!

The state of being joyful is an emotion of elation, bliss, delight, cheerfulness, and a confidence born out of the connection to yourself, to others, to your purpose, and to existence. There is a reason, and you're included in that reason. Being joyful is the result of something else, it is generated by the choice you make, the inputs you choose, and frequently held onto as a desired state of being. It can be intentionally chosen or accidental. Colors, shapes, sounds, smells, tastes and touch are all physical inputs and pleasures that can help develop a state of being joyful. Being joyful as an emotion exists on a continuum, a spectrum, like other emotions from 'a little bit joyful' all the way to extremely, intensely joyful, and yet it is still within you, a state of being for yourself.

I've read that joy is a feeling, an emotion, and that it can be chosen. I have been in the state of being joyful for long periods of time and always enjoy it. I had never once felt the Experience of Joy. It wasn't until I connected internally that I Experienced Joy.

When the state of being joyful crosses over into expanding your sense of self into something more, connecting to yourself, to another, to the universe, then you have Experienced Joy. My experience with Joy is just that, my experience. I'm certain there are small experiences and large experiences only because I have had both. You can too!

Now that we understand the difference between the Experience of Joy and the state of being joyful, let's learn how to have an Experience of Joy!

Connect with the Experience of Joy community at **www.thejoyguy.com**, share your experience!

PART 2

The "Experience of Joy" Game

Opening

Remember as we get into the rules and regulations about playing the game to Experience Joy, if we do not understand clearly where we are we will have no route to plan a trip elsewhere, we will wander aimlessly. The aimless wander is an anomalous state to avoid. However, not all those who wander are lost.

Understanding the warp and wobble of who we are and where we're at, what and who we get to play with and how we play is important. Some of what we are in this moment may be at odds with what we planned, or thought we were intended to be, and some may resonate clearly. With Marie Kondo (www.konmari.com) clarity and purpose we need to identify, evaluate and clarify the what, where, why, how, and when of everything in our lives. Learn to appreciate, to understand the value of, and to resonate with our gameboard, artifacts, and more. It is the basic unit of everything in our lives and knowing the rules and regulations in the present moment is step one. Once we know about the here and now, we can craft a plan to grow into something more.

There are two parts to know about everything – the physical piece, place or person, and the non-physical impact, impression, or feeling. Stuff means something to us, mementos, nostalgia, relationships. One idea to understanding the KonMari Method™: identify the why to the what. 'The what' is on a spectrum from functional to artistic, and also contains an emotional impact.

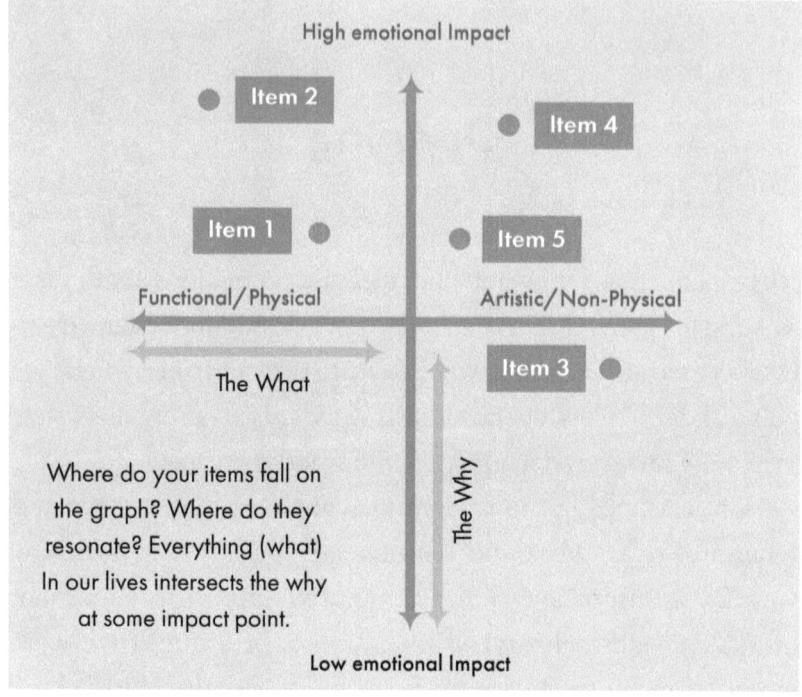

Like a graph, with the horizontal axis going from functional to artistic and the vertical axis being emotional quotient from low to high. Not everything will have favorable ratings but understanding and accepting how we value things in our lives is important.

Let's learn the rules of the game and get started!

Note: Marie Kondo is an inspiration and a joy and has helped millions connect with the joy of tidying. She is the author of the #1 New York Times bestselling book "the life-changing magic of tidying up" and the designer and founder of the KonMari Method™. Connect with Marie at www.konmari.com

PART 2

Chapter 3

The Rules, Objective, Gameboard, Players, Game Pieces, Artifacts, Movement/Play

Rules

There are just two rules. The play of the game is life, and everyone is playing whether they like it, want to, or feel like it. The rules therefore consist of breathing and a heartbeat – two critical playing considerations we will talk a lot about. They are not just the fundamental rules of the game, they are also the fundamental rules of everything. No duh, right? No breath or no heartbeat and your game is over, no restart or second chances. Rather than say 'life' is the name of the game, let's focus on our two basic operating systems – our breathing and heartbeat.

This is the game of Experiencing Joy, so the only other rule is that you accept the end game, having an Experience of

Joy. Without an objective there is no reason to play, and you can continue with simple, easy to obtain, physical pleasure, bliss, delight, even the state of being joyful. There is a lot of it, simple pleasures, and we will learn that as we move around the gameboard we encounter plenty of good things in life, some astronomically good things, and some everyday things that are amazing.

Rule #1: Breathe.

Anyone who is not breathing cannot play this game, although the dead do frequent the gameboard.

A quick Google® search on breathing is revealing:

- "10 Breathing Techniques For Stress Relief And More" – Healthline
- "15 Easy Breathing Techniques To Help You Take 5 Minutes Out Of Your Day To Be Present"
- "8 Deep Breathing Exercises to Reduce Anxiety" - Verywell Mind
- "Stress Management: Breathing Exercises for Relaxation"
- "Breathing Techniques for Stress Relief" – WebMD

Anxiety, Relaxation, Stress, being present - for my entire life I rarely thought about breathing unless I was out of breath, breathing heavy after a run or heavy work. Little did I realize just how important breathing is, and how much it regulates our entire body and ALL the body's operations and processes.

Chapter 3

Our breathing, or Respiratory Rate, sets the pace for ALL of our bodily functions. Metabolism, immunity, plumbing, circulation, endocrine, DNA Maintenance, epigenetics, everything, including our brain and thinking. Through breathing many have achieved incredible physiological changes. Just thinking about what Wim Hoff is able to do boggles my mind at the capacity not only of our bodies but also of our mind and spirit. On June 17th, 2021, Wim Tweeted: "The mind is a neurological muscle that is able to influence your body's molecular system. And if you want this muscle to function optimally, you've got to surrender unconditionally to the experience. You have to really go for it. You have to have the third pillar: mindset." This is The Iceman, known for his ability to control his physiological state through breathing, talking about neuroscience and demonstrating those facts.

It's one thing to physically be able to do something, and another to have the spirit/soul/mind to actually perform it. Breathing is part of the subconscious operation of the body, and by bringing it forward into the conscious we increase our conscious control over our physiology. As Stanford Neuroscientist Andrew Huberman recently asked in a talk he gave "EMDR, medical hypnosis, meditation, talk therapy, holotropic breathing, supplementation, nootropics, drugs – what are the behavioral interventions that allow people to adjust their state?" Huberman goes on to talk about changing our internal state, our physiological state, using conscious physical activities - and in this case breathing. Huberman categorizes breathing into 3 categories – inhale focused, exhale focused, and balanced – and points out that we can intentionally take conscious control over an unconscious process and thereby change our internal state – by breathing. (Andrew Huberman, 2020). This is a neuroscientist talking about breathing.

The importance of breathing is brought out by the coherence of neuroscientific research (Huberman, et al) and practical application (Wim Hoff, et al). Scientifically we know that we can regulate our internal state, our physiological state which includes our emotions as well as our physicality by breathing, and the practical application by The Iceman shows us the potentiality. Breathing is hugely important and life altering. Learning how to use our breathing consciously adds to our power level!

Rule #2: Have a Heartbeat.

I was reading The Science of the Heart by the HeartMath Institute (HMI) (Institute, 2019) and at a certain point I wrote in the margin, "There's magic in the gaps." What came to me in the reading was that there is information in the spaces between things, between events, in the silence, the pause, the blank space, the gap. I had always considered it just that – empty space. What I learned is that it isn't just empty space, there is information in that space, in the gap. There is magic in the gap. The rest in music, the pause in dramatics, section breaks, chapter breaks, even paragraph changes. Artists call it 'timing.' All sorts of gaps began to become apparent and gain importance, but one that really impacted me is Heart Rate Variability – the change in the gaps between heartbeats. (The HeartMath Institute, 2021) The space between heartbeats is not uniform, it varies slightly. This variation in the amount of time between heartbeats – the gaps - is your HRV, Heart Rate Variability. I like this article from Harvard Health Publishing:

"People who have a high HRV may have greater cardio-vascular fitness and be more resilient to stress. HRV may also provide personal feedback about your lifestyle and help motivate those who are considering taking steps toward a healthier life. It is fascinating to see how HRV changes as you incorporate more mindfulness, meditation, sleep, and especially physical activity into your life. For those who love data and numbers, this can be a nice way to track how your nervous system is reacting not only to the environment, but also to your emotions, thoughts, and feelings." (Campos MD, 2019)

We all know that without a heartbeat we have little chance of life, but we give little credit to the cadence of our heart. The heart's rhythm – the beats, the pauses, the rests, the gaps – the music our heart plays vibrates, and generates a much larger influence than simply providing circulatory beats.

Objective

The objective is simple and plain: to have an Experience of Joy. While it would be nice to be able to simply walk into the experience like going out to dinner or seeing a movie, there are complications that interfere with the Joy Experience. Those complications create dissonance internally and externally, and that dissonance hampers the ability to Experience of Joy by making us discordant. Dissonance is a conflict between views, for example loving the color pink but disbelieving you look good in pink. Marketing uses cognitive dissonance to make us feel awkward that we don't have something

– their something, on sale now! Having conflicting views is dissonant, and it can be mild to extreme. We might say the objective is to remove dissonance within us in order to create a coherent environment to Experience Joy. I won't talk much about what causes dissonance – there is just too much and what a depressing book that would be. Instead, I will focus on how we can create coherence, resonance, and purposely prepare the mind, body, soul, and spirit for the Experience of Joy.

Gameboard

The area of play is the environment of our lives: Our id/ego, our home, our transportation, our yard, the park, the fields, the mountains, the garden, the places you eat, the places you worship, the gym, the commute. You might be in school, in a care facility, in jail. The board of play is alive, constantly in flux, changing, and there are parts we know nothing about. Recent technology and scientific discoveries show the nature of the gameboard may be more than what we think, see, or experience, both in content and context. Additional research shows us that we can influence the game board with as little as a Butterfly Effect (Vernon, 2017) or as great as a regional sports team blasting into championships after regional disasters. (Boren, 2017) Gameboard changes are real, can be intentional, and have unlimited potential.

The gameboard we have is often not of our choosing. Even late into life it can be dictated by family, finances, and career. Whatever it is, it is, and this is the playing area, our gameboard. It does not matter what gameboard you have. If you cannot learn to resonate where you are you will never be able to resonate anywhere. Playing the game where you're at is an essential skill and a fundamental ability.

The gameboard is not static, and there are a huge variety of changes that occur sometimes minute by minute. We can influence our gameboard by simply taking a drive, and sometimes just driving can resonate with us. How many parents drive their kids to sleep not knowing but somehow feeling that the vibrations are resonating with their child? I love driving. I am learning how to resonate with traffic.

Learn how to resonate with your gameboard and power up!

Players

You, family, school mates, friends, co-workers, cousins, uncles, aunts, neighbors, idols (movie, music, & muses), authors, the people who support causes you support, your teammates, your tribe, or tribes. The players proceed in the gameboard environment at a constant rate as if in a canoe, using the paddle to change course in real time with incremental strokes. Every interaction and exchange increases your resonance and adds to your personal power level.

Other people are playing, although sometimes I'm not sure what game they're playing, or if they're even on the same gameboard. (Religions and Politics, for example) The people on your gameboard are critically important. There is common knowledge that we are the average of the 5 people or couples that are our closest associates. Research into quantum molecular mechanics now shows that our neural network helps explain why. Much like a computer network with computers as nodes on the network, we have a connected mental neural network with our friends and close associates. If you've ever been on a team that clicked well, where you knew what the teammate on your left and right were going to do, with a confidence that was more than simple faith, the neuroscientists are now saying that was participation in a neural network among a group. The brains, thought patterns, energy levels, attitudes, and more from the people around you share a neural connection in real time. Coherence enhances power, and discordance destroys power.

Understand your neural network connection to others and power up!

Game pieces

Your clothes, jewelry, scents and shoes, pen and pencil, notebook, journal, backpack, your wallet, your purse, your tools, sports equipment, your car, truck, or bike. Your food, water, sanitation devices. With nonstop buy and trade rarely does 24 hours go by without our artifact pieces changing. Throughout the game we pick up and put down various pieces with a Marie Condo KonMari™ question "does this physical thing bring me joy?" Pieces/artifacts are important to completing who we are, and as we learn that everything vibrates with its own wavelength or frequency (all material and non-material things) we search for artifacts that resonate with us. Your individuality also has a vibration, a resonance, a frequency, and when you resonate with a game piece that game piece's resonance adds to your power level!

Artifacts

We have stones, necklaces, rings, bracelets with charms, talismans, and more that all resonate with us at a corporal and a quantum level. Books, clothes, coasters on the table, and the cups and glasses we use. Pictures on the wall, tapestries, accent walls. We have artifacts at home, school, and work. That's why we have them. There is a resonance not only in the materials, or corporal substance, but also in the shape, size, color, cut, style, etc. Matching your adornment to your resonance is a power up success!

The variety of things we look at, touch, taste, smell is immense and changes within and between cultures, and all only present physical pleasure to us. They are nice to look at, eat, drive, play, listen to, wear, and they can add to our being joyful, to our power level. Feng Shui, Interior Design, and Fashion are just a few of the many industries that intentionally surround us with artifacts.

Resonate with the artifacts in your life and power up!

Movement/play

Play proceeds at will and can be done in increments, moments, minutes, chunks, hours, mealtimes, parts of a day, whole days, weeks, months, years, decades, lifetimes. Time is also under scientific scrutiny, but for all of us in this time we travel in the same flow, the same cohort/generation/tribe, moving at a constant speed. I have experienced time gaps, skips, and elongation, and seen the bogus 'time traveler' videos by @unicosobreviviente (only survivor). I still only have one personal rate of flow, unwavering and sometimes frustrating. Hindsight is 20/20, and The HeartMath Institute has discovered we know things before they happen, or that our heart knows and tells our brain. (Institute, 2019) The stream we paddle on is a constant flow, even across rapids, obstacles, and threats. Sometimes 'jumps' occur, where time is shortened, new skills are learned quickly and your ability 'jumps' forward. Time is a strange thing, but as much as we move around, we also are 'moving' in time.

In the game of Experiencing Joy movement is particularly important. Active participation is required to consciously work towards and accept the results of Experiencing Joy. Once you have an Experience of Joy you will always be able to experience it again. While we move about in our daily tasks there are activities we can incorporate to increase our ability to experience Joy. Once we figured out that working out is good for us we gave birth to an $87 billion dollar global fitness center industry (Stasha, 2021), and a $4.5 Trillion dollar wellness industry.

Hundreds of millions of people are striving for the right movement, spa, and activity that will help them move forward, something that resonates with them. The runner's high, the physical buzz of a good lifting session. I recently learned to connect to my heart in a more blended conscious manner, and immediately saw my whole circulatory system in a simple, elegant, red and blue diagram inside me, and my capillaries started tingling, all over, all at once. I had never tried that before and have been only partly successful since. I continue to move, try, and practice what worked for me or for others. I get coaching, instruction, and mentorship online, in person, and by reading. The level I am at each moment is transitionary and will continue to change. Without direct effort applied the second law of thermodynamics tells me the change will be a reduction, a loss. I must apply effort to move forward, to power up and then to level up.

Learn The Rules, Objective, Gameboard, Players, Game Pieces, Artifacts, Movement/Play and Power up!

Connect with the Experience of Joy community at **www.thejoyguy.com**, share your experience!

PART 2

Chapter 4
Power ups, Level Ups, and Bonuses

These include anything and everything you do to build coherence, a connection. When you see something that is beautiful and connect with it, what part of you recognizes what part(s) of the beauty? Is it the color, shape, style, size, majesty, grandeur, sound, taste, feel? Your *reaction* to the input. Do you feel it in your head, your heart, your gut, your spirit? Where does it vibrate, resonate with you? As you identify why you appreciate the sight, sound, object, experience, or feeling connect with two things: yourself and your reason, both corporal and ethereal. And then learn how to deepen that connection between your senses.

Perhaps you're wondering, "What is connecting with what, it's all the same thing." True story, it is all about you. No joke, no pun. This is how *you* power up. Your reason is yourself, and there is no implication of anything else. Whether we are talking about you, your mind, brain, heart, soul, gut, instinct, genes, or spirit it is all about you and what you connect with. You may see something that creates a feeling. *Why* did you get that feeling? I am not asking where you felt it, or what your physiological reaction was to the inputs, why did you react? What part, literally what part, of the input and what part of you reacted? Make that connection, resonate with those two things going on inside you.

When we learn to connect with what resonates with us there will be things in our lives that just do not resonate, they are discordant. Just understand the rules of the universe, resonance enhances power, discordance destroys power. The US Congress is unfortunately a great example. We can see that when there is coherence, more gets done. Same in our lives, within us individually and as part of a group of any size. I have been in many situations in my life when I was coherent with the group and had great success, and also times when there was discordance, and utterly and completely failed. Big events, life events, small things – everything works better in coherence. I've heard it called Flow – a complete absorption into a thought or activity. Psychology Today tells us that "It involves intense focus, creative engagement, and the loss of awareness of time and self." (Psychology Today Staff, 2021)

Joy connects you. When you experience the overwhelming expansion of your heart and soul you feel connected to the world in a greater way. Some call it connecting to the Divine, some call it connecting to Gaia. Research is going on right now to show that our coherence impacts the global resonance of the planet. (Institute, 2019) Power up when you make a connection!

My entire life my favorite color has been blue, like my eyes. Recently I was going through the Marie Diamond system and re-organizing my vision board. (Diamond, 2017) Blue is prominent, *in my health and wellness*. Red is my success color. This makes greater sense when I look back (20/20 hindsight) and see how healthy I have been my entire life and continue to this day. I was frequently dressed in blue, never in red. I knew when I read that in Marie's book that it was true, Red – albeit still not my favorite – resonated as my success color, and I am changing some of my game pieces/artifacts to Red. I look forward to greater success, in my finances, career, relationships, capacity to give as well as to receive, to love and be loved.

Be wary of the symbols in your life. A dozen years ago I had to sell my blue Mazda and started driving a Red Toyota. Shortly after that success began to come back into my life. The first Red Toyota was sold for what I bought it for after driving it for 5 years, and I bought my second Red Toyota, upgrading 16 model years. 6 years driving that red car I was promoted, successfully finished my bachelor's degree, worked two jobs, and moved into a more senior level position. I then bought my current Blue Mazda and had a career change. Symbols are important.

The connections I made gave me a power up. And it was both a corporal and ethereal gain. In the next section we'll talk a little about the difference between the physical and non-physical, corporal -vs- ethereal.

0.1 Corporeal Power ups

These are the physical, or corporal, senses, and you should be familiar with them. Your vision, also known as your sight, hearing or auditory, taste, sometimes called gustatory, touch or tactile sensations, and smell or olfactory recognition. Pathways.org talks of two other senses to bring the total to 7, the vestibular and proprioception senses. These make sense to me, but I was never aware of them. (Pun intended.)

The vestibular sense is your sense of movement and balance, and this lets us know if we are moving in an elevator, and proprioception is your sense of body position, or body organization. This is what lets us know, reflexively, what to protect in and around our bodies, and explains why we raise our hands to protect our head or our body when we sense or recognize danger. While vestibular sense may present us with claustrophobia and be the target of carnival rides, our 'body sense' is what allows us to "crack an egg while not crushing the egg in our hands." (Pathways.org, 2020) (7senses.org.au, 2020)

Understanding our senses allows us to connect to them and use them in concert. When I was in restaurant management, I would teach my servers that the customers always ate in order of sight, smell, and taste. (Sometimes smell, sight, taste.) This is true of food as well as many other consumer goods. Senses are not normally soloists, and the more we connect multiple senses the more we're coherent with ourselves. Do you have physical memories that share two or more senses? Is the memory more intense or detailed the more senses are involved? When trying to imprint a memory, stamp it with all that you can. Physical feeling, emotions, sights, sounds, smells. Become familiar with your senses and learn to fully sense where you are as often as you can.

These are the physical, or corporeal, aspects of your playing piece moving through the gameboard of life. The rules that apply here are mostly simple – you can't see with your ears, for example. Sometimes things can be mixed, such as taste and smell, touch and proprioception, and then there are those who tell us we have non-physical senses. If you have ever felt Déjà vu, gotten goosebumps, or 'knew in your gut/heart' about something, then you might have experienced a physiological response to a non-physical, or ethereal, sense.

> **Try This!** Recall a memory of a pleasant event and enhance it. While recalling the memory, remember more details like smells, tastes, or sounds. Think how your body felt, intensify the emotions, and then resave the memory. Ink it in. Create associations with other memories. You've just changed your brain!

Resonate with to your physical, corporal senses and Power up!

0.5 Ethereal Power ups

This is defined, wonderfully clearly, as "not of the body." This means that when we 'love' in our hearts, 'thrill' at the accomplishment, have Déjà vu or a 'gut' feeling we are experiencing an ethereal sense or event that produces a conscious, corporal, physiological response.

> **Try This!** Remember a particularly sour taste you've had, like a really sour lemon slice. The tartness and juiciness causing your mouth to pucker. If you had ANY physical response to that thought, then you can recall a memory and re-feel the experience. Memories re-live the experience.

The ethereal senses are associated with four memories: the mind, the soul, the instinct, and the spirit. The mind is a no brainer – we all know we have memory in the brain that our mind can access and recall. Our hearts remember things our soul feels – all the passions and all the virtues. Our instinct has been shown to come from the heart and I wonder if our gut has the same connection as the heart. While we have heart transplants and can observe the results, we do not at this point have gut transplants. (But they do poop transfers. Don't worry – there's a pill for that.) Memory transplants? It has been suggested that as completely corporal beings with nothing ethereal we could 'of course' transplant memory into another, or into a database. I disagree that we are simply physical, and that Artificial Intelligence can replicate human complexity and depth. Would the machine have a fear of death at being unplugged? To whom would they look to for help in preventing or forestalling such a death? There is more to who we are than the sum of the parts.

"However, several scientists subscribe to an alternative theory, believing that memory could also be stored in epigenetic information via RNA transcription. If true, the concept of transferring a stored memory in the form of an RNA sequence could be transferred to a different host." (Hoshide, MD, MPH & Jandial, MD, PhD, 2018) The 'memory' the scientists 'transplanted' seemed to me to be a simple autogenic response. Not necessarily what we might call a memory, but more of a reflexive, stimulus-response activity. While this "memory" may be able to be tracked, isolated, and transplanted the intensity is a question for me. Referring back to the spectrum, or the continuum that is the range of intensity of just being joyful - is the memory just assigned a number and then forever only has that assigned numerical intensity? The challenge I have with that is talking about an event you were at and finding another who was at the same event. The compounding of memories can change the intensity number – good or bad – through the shared neural connection creating neural plasticity. The AI function would be a computed standard, but we all know there is nothing standard about interacting with someone and recalling life.

When we get inputs from our senses to be processed, whether it's from the eyes, ears, nose, mouth, or skin our physical corporal brain processes the facts and information, and our mind decides how to handle the input. Recent research by the HeartMath Institute (HMI) actually shows that our heart senses – intuits – information 4.8 seconds before the event and sends a message to the brain 3.5 seconds before sensory input, and HMI postulates that the heart actually told the brain what to expect and how to feel about and process the input. (McCraty PhD, 2015) This tells me why I dread when nothing has happened yet. My heart alerts my brain about the input before I get the sensory input. If we knew how to focus our awareness on this intuitive process we could develop an acutely aware intuition, an ethereal 'not of the body' conscious sense of what's coming next.

While we have a growing body of scientific evidence for the heart-mind connection, less is known about the gut instinct, or 'a feeling' in your gut. Ever have butterflies in your stomach? A shrinking sensation, goosebumps, or even a sudden onset of insight or clarity? According to Healthline (Robertson PhD, 2020) our gut is connected to the brain via the Vagus nerve, and it communicates back and forth as if in constant conversation both physically and biochemically.

(Not sure why biochemically is separate from physical.) Robertson goes on to say that the gut 'may' influence the brain.' I agree, based on personal experience with my own gut. I've also had the experience of my gut communicating with my entire body, when I have been extremely 'calorie poor' and my body reacts before my mind catches up to tell me to eat.

The ethereal parts of our body simply refer to those elements of us that we are all familiar with but can't be surgically operated on. The ethereal, non-physical parts of us can be consciously directed, recognized, enjoyed, influenced, and changed. Even our hereditary genetic spirit can be influenced – enhanced or diminished – intentionally.

Connect to the 'not of the body' ethereal parts of you and power up!

Extra Power Up

There is magic in the gaps, both ethereal and corporal. The space between, the pause, the rest, the hesitation, the quiet before the storm. In researching this book information from The HeartMath Institute showed me that gaps between heartbeats vary, and this heart rate variation is an indicator of many things in the body. (The HeartMath Institute, 2021) When reviewing what I read I felt there was magic in the gaps. This revelation broadened, and in conversations with others it expanded.

In a speech or even a conversation, pauses create impact and dramatic effect. In music the gaps create the beat, the tempo, the cadence for the score. When composing the rests are programmed and included as part of the composition. It is the gap that insulates, that allows another to speak, or to respond. The space between allows growth and development in the garden, and in our everyday lives as we sleep, taking a gap to regroup, refresh, rejuvenate, and repair. The nap – the quintessential gap in the day.

When a newborn naps on our chest in between fits of exploration and discovery we revel, rejoice, and feel our heart-field joined to another in an expansive expression of love, peace, and enlightenment provided only by a parental connection. There is magic in this gap.

In the space between beats, we live our lives, peppered with staccato actions. As science discovers more and more about existence, they grow in astonishment at just how much empty space there is in matter, the stuff we think of as solid, continuous, and without gaps. In the gaps between bits in bytes data knows where to go and how to perform. (If they could vary those gaps could the byte then hold an infinite number of bits?) In the space between start and finish we insert many other beats, actions, and seemingly multitask. In the gap we have accidents and tragedies, regret and guilt. Resonating with the space between is a connecting action, a power up. The gaps far outweigh the beats, exponentially, unimaginably large is the space between, immense, and developing coherence with even a small section is an enlargement of persona, id, ego. Power up and know that you can connect to the beat *and* connect to the gap. There is magic in the gaps.

You are connected - coherent - with your physical and non-physical you! Power up to 0.2!

Connect with the Experience of Joy community at **www.thejoyguy.com**, share your experience!

PART 3

Internal Coherence

Opening

Connection is the pathway to Experiencing Joy, and connecting to self, becoming coherent, is the first step. Once you are coherent with your id/ego, you can then use conscious intention to Experience Joy.

This is where we all start. We are all start out as a unit of one, one person, an individual animated within physical existence - a cognitive and emotional being. Understanding our corporal, or physical, and ethereal, or non-physical existence allows us to learn how to resonate as one whole, an incredibly powerful single unit.

There are two parts everyone has, and we need to learn how they resonate – the corporal and the ethereal. When we talk about the corporal, we are referring to the physical; for example the Brain, the Heart, the Gut, and our Genes. When we refer to the ethereal, we're talking about the intangible - lacking material substance - but within our corporal existence definitely having material influence. The Mind describes the ethereal portion of the brain, the Soul the ethereal part of the heart, the Instinct the intangible part of our Gut, and our Spirit the non-physical part of our heredity, or our Genes. Experiencing Joy is a resonance of our corporal and ethereal existence. It is the combining of our two parts – the beat and the gap - into a resonating whole. The guitar with the strings, the piano with the player, the Ying with the Yang.

There has been some great research in the field of resonance, coherence, and entrainment in some areas and very little in others. We know there is a connection between the heart and brain, between the gut and the brain, and I think it almost goes without saying our genes are connected to everything. To see what happens in synchronization, look up on You Tube, "spontaneous synchronization metronomes" and what you will see is 5 random metronomes that are on a platform start to resonate in sync and match beats. There is another video with a lot of metronomes and the same thing happens. Or look for "Pendulum wave machine" and watch with curiosity how balls of identical construction but hanging at different lengths move between synchronization and independence, discordance. Connecting our body and senses creates synchronization, flow, and resonance. It operates in the same way within us to the swinging balls, where we have times of independence, perhaps some times of chaos, and then times of synchronicity, and the synchronicity can vary from a little, to some, to complete.

When we connect our corporal and ethereal existence and learn how to resonate with them we will enter into a state in which we can Experience Joy. Don't be surprised by the Experience, revel in it. Make your Joy Experience better with your conscious participation. We have the power to create. As you begin to create your incoming environment, go for Experiencing Joy and know that you can succeed. It will change your life.

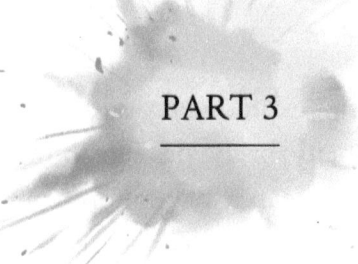

PART 3

Chapter 5

The Mind – Brain Resonance

The Mind-Brain Resonance

We're all familiar with the brain, and some know more about the brain than others regarding the structure, content, ingredients, and functions. The brain is one of the most widely studied and photographed organs in the body. Up to 95% of it operates sub-consciously, running all of our systems in the body we rarely think about consciously. It is when we recognize the subconscious operation of our brain and become as familiar as possible with that powerful 95% we power up, gain advantage, and begin to develop conscious cognition.

In 1826 Jean Anthelme Brillat-Savarin wrote "Tell me what you eat and I will tell you what you are." Today we are learning that we are not only what we *think* we are, but also who we *remember* we are.

Recent research has exploded around the brain, and what they call neural plasticity, or the proven ability of the brain to change, to develop, to heal, is at the forefront. The physical structure that is the operations center of our corporal existence had been thought to be static and what you got is all you got. So much for past medicinal doctrine in this area. I guess that's why they call it practicing medicine! Further research is replicating evidence about how the 5% of our conscious thought impacts neural plasticity and creates change in our brain. When we think, what we think changes our brain, changes who we are. Be intentional about your neural plasticity!

The Brain, although about 95% subconscious, is influenced by our thoughts, our mind. We gather inputs and then decide in our mind what action to take, and those actions over time change our brain. I imagine that when I was born my brain was like a huge empty library. Over time volumes (colors, shapes, textures, sounds, smells, tastes, motion) were added to my library and filed appropriately, mostly. And as more volumes – books, magazines, videos, activities, relationships, experiences, etc. – were added to my library by the sensory inputs of sounds, sights, tastes, smells, touches, up/down, backward/forward, sideways, neuroplastic connections were created, and associations and relationships with existing entries developed. *The associations that a new entry can make are only with previously existing entries.* The existing entries in my library did not have the connections to the new entry before the new entry was created. When the new entry came in, <u>my brain changed.</u> My brain's neural plasticity created new connections, associations, and relationships. This is basic neural plasticity functionality. Frequently, we consciously think of the connection, or the relationship to something we already know or believe. This is the conscious direction of neural plasticity - the ability to intentionally change our brain by creating conscious connections. Consciously add a new volume to your library and the connections your mind (ethereal) makes to other volumes in your brain (corporal) creates new physical connections in your brain. It changes your brain. What you think changes your brain.

Bonus Power Up! The neural plastic activity on your brain is not laser focused. Your brain increases blood and nutrient flow to the brain in general as well as specifically, and there is collateral improvement as well as the new brain cell growth. Learn something new! Grow your brain!

The mind, or our thoughts, are never thought to be subconscious at all. Conscious cognition of planning, organizing, complex reasoning, prioritizing, and synthesis of thought are considered to require conscious effort. Simple stimulus-response-type actions are all that the subconscious mind handles, such as reflexive actions, although I am not sure I would classify the operation of my body as 'simple stimulus-response,' it actually is. The process of cellular respiration, protein manufacture *for specific varied purposes*, digestion that takes what's needed for now and a little bit more for later and discards the rest, my immunity, even the waste disposal from all those cellular processes going on simultaneously billions of times per second in my body are in no way simple, although I agree that most is stimulus-response generated. I eat, therefore I digest; I breathe, therefore I oxygenate, subconsciously. Conscious thought directs the upright, ambulatory operation, and for only using 5% of the brain we can do some amazing things. Learning how to direct our conscious thought has been the focus of a thousand books or more (How many times have you seen something telling you how to 'Think'?), millions of conversations ('I think that....'), and countless motivational seminars. (Thank you, Tony Robbins. (Tony Robbins, 2021) The choice you made and continue to follow through on has made people better.) By connecting our consciousness to our subconsciousness and changing the balance of power between the conscious and subconscious we can intentionally, purposefully, change our brain. Talk about powering up!

Brain Memory

The brain has neurons, neurotransmitters, and memory. For most people I've ever met the brain is the focal point of activity, ability, and memory. The brain has also been pegged as our biggest obstacle. The ability to focus and stay on task, to create and start something new, set and follow goals, deal with distractions, squirrels, sparks and spittle's are all associated with our brain and how we think. The automatic mechanical body functions we give no account to, and little credit to even their subconscious existence except when they demand it. The vast majority of our mind's activity is associated with memory. We learn how to do something, add that volume to our library, create the associations, and then repeat based on that memory.

When we learn something new and add that to our memory library, we engage neural plasticity: we change our brain using neural plasticity. When we recall a memory and enhance or relive the memory: we consciously direct neural plasticity. Associate this memory with that sense, idea, feeling. We can create new associations, new relationships in our brain. Our mind, ethereal conscious thought, changes our brain, the physical corporal being. The physical corporal brain is a vast library of information that has many mysteries.

Brain Mystery! How did we 'learn' how to digest? Pump our heart, breathe, build our immunity, filter our blood, and more? These are believed to be genetic instructions included with our DNA blueprint, our genetic ancestry or human heredity. Not just the instructions, but the entire system construction, organization, and operation. WOW! No wonder the DNA strand is so big!

Connect the mind and the brain and increase to Power Level 0.3!

Connect with the Experience of Joy community at **www.thejoyguy.com**, share your experience!

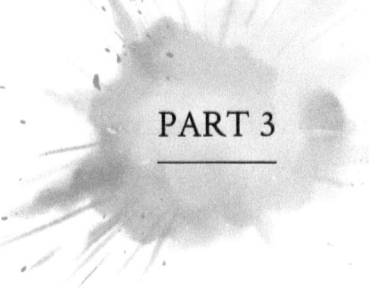

PART 3

Chapter 6

The Heart – Soul Resonance

Heart-Soul Resonance

What if our heart was the actual brain of the body? What if the brain was just a processing center, taking sensory inputs (directed by our mind) and processing them for action or storage? Remember the HeartMath Institute has already shown the connection between the heart and the brain; and given insight into intuition being knowledge in the heart of what's going to take place next many seconds in advance. Connecting to your heart will give you greater insight, more experiences of Déjà vu, a powerful resonance, and increased resilience. (Institute, 2019) In addition to heart functions, the heart also has memory – neurons and neurotransmitters, and a large, strong, electromagnetic field.

I think the Soul exists as our heart's electromagnetic field, so much bigger than our corporal heart, and able to connect to, see, feel, and experience the gameboard, players, artifacts, and more *before* our corporal senses. When we're connected to our heart and soul the feeling is expansive and lush, coherent and full, flowing outward and renewing. The resonance can be intense, secure, a common and familiar combination of the corporal and ethereal. In love we feel the warmth of another field, another soul, and with love we resonate with another. This is a 2.0 Power Level experience! When the heart-soul within you joins with the heart-soul of another it is one of the most powerful power ups we can realize.

The soul is our quantum connection to the created or physical world, as well as the unseen or ethereal. Our heart field as our soul permeates our existence like Pigpen's™ cloud, it surrounds us, and we know instantly when our soul connects. When our soul touches something or someone the feeling of connection is both corporal and ethereal. Our soul can ache, rejoice, and love. The music that resonates, food that satiates, the rumble, purr, or caw of an animal, the smell of... (Bacon? Flowers? Lemon? Idaho Blue Spruce? Mint? Patchouli? It's called aromatherapy and everyone does it, just a few do it purposefully, intentionally, consciously.) The soul has the ability to sense, to see, and to feel in ways we know and understand and in ways we don't, both meaningful and impactful. Whether we accept it or not, our soul is bigger than just our body; we can feel it. Our soul has frequency and substance, impacts our existence and what we resonate with.

Heart Memory

The heart has neurons and neurotransmitters, is considered to function independently, and have memory. We now understand the heart knows; how exactly we are not really sure, but there is a lot of conjecture and wonder. It's possible that our heart's electromagnetic field is involved. Connecting to your heart has also been the subject of literature, conferences, retreats, and more. If the heart knows before the brain, would being connected to your heart make you prescient? Would it increase your vision, give access to a broader band of the electromagnetic spectrum? The heart's neural connection to the brain is enlightening, understanding the heart has independent operating capacity is reassuring, but the most surprising revelation is the heart has memory.

The heart having memory may not impress you but consider that our memories impact our daily lives and existence. ("We are what we remember we are.") Some even say that our perceived reality is solely based on our memories, that the reality we see and experience is only real because we remember it. It is true that we resonate in the present moment as a result of all that has played out before in our lives. That's just fact, we can't be a product of what isn't there. If we exist as a compilation of past experiences, then our heart's memory is very important. Investigations into the memory of the heart are ongoing, with the experiences of heart transplant patients informing scientists.

The statements and implications of this 2019 study request on PubMed are informative:

Abstract
Personality changes following heart transplantation, **which have been reported for decades,** include accounts of recipients acquiring the personality characteristics of

their donor. Four categories of personality changes are discussed in this article: (1) changes in preferences, (2) alterations in emotions/temperament, **(3) modifications of identity,** and **(4) memories from the donor's life**. The acquisition of donor personality characteristics by recipients following heart transplantation is hypothesized to occur via the **transfer of cellular memory**, and *four types of cellular memory* are presented: **(1) epigenetic memory, (2) DNA memory, (3) RNA memory, and (4) protein memory.** Other possibilities, such as the transfer of memory via intracardiac neurological memory and energetic memory, are discussed as well. Implications for the future of heart transplantation are explored including the importance of reexamining our current definition of death, studying how the transfer of memories might affect the integration of a donated heart, determining whether memories can be transferred via the transplantation of other organs, and investigating which types of information can be transferred via heart transplantation. Further research is recommended. (Liester, 2019) **[Emphasis mine.]**

What they are seeing in some heart transplant patients and searching for more experimental data on is that our identity, emotions, and memories exist in our heart. To such an extent as to change the recipient's embodied cognition through a physical heart transplant. When the heart is moved, the previous owner's identity, emotions, and memories are sometimes transplanted as well. The memory has been identified as genetic (DNA), epigenetic (DNA management), protein (heart muscle), and RNA (DNA operations).

Anyone who's ever learned how to ride a bike has experienced muscle memory. Once you know how, once you've added that volume to your memory library, you've got it for life with little conscious thought. Once we've trained our muscles they can operate reflexively or 'revert to the training.' It's also been called cellular memory. Whatever it may be called the existence of memory in our heart – good and bad memories – is real. The cells of the heart muscles remember, within the proteins, the DNA, RNA, and Epigenetically.

Connect to your heart and allow your soul freedom. Recognize the heart's electromagnetic field extends out 9 to 12 feet in all directions, a spheric field of power that connects and attracts. Accept and receive the power from others, from their smile, laughter, and love.

Feel the power of your heart and soul and Power Up to Power Level 0.5!

Connect with the Experience of Joy community at **www.thejoyguy.com**, share your experience!

PART 3

Chapter 7

The Gut – Instinct Resonance

The Gut – Instinct Resonance

Adrenaline is released by our Adrenal Glands, which sit directly on top of our kidneys, in response to a fight, flight, or freeze situation. The hormones released increase our heart rate and blood pressure. One reason is to signal the body that it needs to take more nutrients from the gut and transfer them to where they are needed – urgently. This includes our conscious processing center, the brain, and also our muscles and other operating and sensory organs.

We know from recent research by HMI that the heart knows before the brain, and we know the heart tells the brain. We don't know if the heart also tells the gut on the way to telling the brain. Something about loose bowels soiling pants being a common colloquialism in fight, flight, or freeze situations comes to mind. Is it really butterflies in our stomach, or more likely instinctual memory fluttering? Just what is it that signals the adrenals? Is there really a sensory alarm the brain processes from inputs and then alerts the adrenals? Or does the heart, perhaps even informed by the soul, tell the endocrine system on the way to the brain, in the gap between sensing and the brain getting the info. Remember the magic in the gaps. I'm trying to remember if I was ready, physically, to fight, flee, or freeze and waiting for the instant the brain decided which to do. I think we need more research to confirm.

The vagus nerve pathway shows the communication between the gut and the brain is constant, and most of this occurs in our subconscious as we rely on our brain to operate our bodily functions subconsciously. When the corporal function of the gut transcends into the ethereal, we call that our gut instinct. When it happens in absence of prior experience to draw from that's called instinctual memory. How many times have you experienced the impact of your adrenals *before* you had seen, heard, or smelled danger? Has worry ever impacted you? Worry feels like a blow to the gut. Not the mental confusion about what you're going to do, the worry about consequences. Your gut has power.

Gut Memory

New research is establishing the link between our microbiome in our gut and our brain.

> "While the digestive tract and the brain feel far apart in your body, they are actually connected via a 24/7 direct line of biochemical communication, set up by special nerve

cells and immune pathways. It's called the gut-brain axis. Down in the gut, bacteria make neuroactive compounds, including 90% of our neurotransmitter serotonin, which regulate our emotions." (Wanucha, 2018)

Wait, did they say 90% of our serotonin is produced in the gut? Give me the recipe for that! What foods can I eat to enhance serotonin production? If we do eat by what we see, smell, and taste is it any wonder cooking can be so rewarding? Did I already talk about taste? We are not only what we eat, we also experience what we eat, in our gut, via the gut-brain axis. All the nutrients needed for the brain, the heart, the gut, and the genes are produced by the gut. The brain, although subconsciously – I eat, therefore I digest – knows what's going on. All the time.

Ask any chef/cook about the power of food and they will wax poetic. We have a sign in our kitchen, "If you feed them, they will come." How many associate food with love, acceptance, self-worth, reward, and in general get or have gotten emotional about food? How much love has come out of the kitchen? How much Joy? There's real power here; it's your gut. Your microbiome has macro power!

I was preparing (mise en place) breakfast in the kitchen in Sedona Arizona on a glorious morning in the dessert. In the soft amber lightening of the day well before sunrise Steve Hampton was playing guitar. As the cook, I was just chopping potatoes and veggies for breakfast potatoes. I resonated deeply with where I was, what I was doing, what I was seeing, and what I was smelling and hearing; I had an Experience of Joy.

Recognizing the beginning of the Experience, the expansion, I also recognized where this one came from, my gut. I set my knife down and looked up, closed my eyes, breathed in and captured the memory and then walked out to the patio. (Consciously wanting to add to the memory, the Experience.) I breathed in the sights, sounds, smells with an expansive smile and impression: imprint tattoo.

A study has found that healing energy comes from our gut. "On investigating the source of this energy Green discovered that the pulses were coming from the healers abdomen, called *dan tien* and considered the central engine of internal energy in the body in Chinese martial arts." (McTaggert, 2008) The gut is important, and we take it for granted, subconsciously never giving it a second thought until it acts up. We have a symbiotic relationship within our gut that is energetic and powerful. We want to resonate with the gut's importance, and value its strength.

The gut has up to 2 ½ times as many neurons and neurotransmitters as the heart and is the main source of nutrients powering our corporal existence. This concentration of brain cells in our intestines indicates the gut is not only connected to the brain but is also one of the memory storage rooms in our library. The gut is in operation 24/7 with digestion responsibilities, and food digestion has an impact on our emotions, our gut, our brain, and the entire symbiosis within. There is communication between the brain and the gut we know, and I think there is communication between the heart and the gut. My taste has fleeting to no memory, but I go back to where I've eaten tasty food before. Food and food event memories are in my gut, and when I think of a great tasting food, I access what the taste was like – in my gut, which is in constant communication with my brain, where I am only slightly conscious and way too subconscious.

Connect with your gut and Power Up to Power Level 0.7!

Connect with the Experience of Joy community at **www.thejoyguy.com**, share your experience!

PART 3

Chapter 8

The Genes – Spirit Resonance

The Genetic – Spirit Resonance

We are what our ancestry says we are, sometimes blended with new information but still no escape from the reality of what we're built with – some combination of the DNA of our parents, who were some combination of their parents. One strand of DNA contains a gigantic amount of data, and we start out as a pure distillation of what created our physical bodies, the DNA in the sperm mixed with the DNA in the egg. The divinity of conception resulting in new creation, the miracle of birth genetic blending.

From that initial blending of DNA we grow into adult humans influenced by Nature and Nurture. Epigenetics states that external and internal factors have been identified that influence internal gene expression. While there is some debate on whether or not epigenetic gene expressions may be inheritable, it is accepted that our genes are intentionally and unintentionally changed with internal and external inputs, and that our corporal and ethereal environment – part of the gameboard – influence our genes as well. There is a growing body of knowledge that indicates some epigenetic changes our parents incurred *are* inherited, and that we have the ability to improve our genetic legacy for our children, both in the DNA given by nature and in development by nurturing, from birth to death. (Birth to Transcendence/Transformation?) Our nurture continues through life, and as nurture gives way to experience both have potential to change both our brains and DNA.

The Experience of Joy changes us! It traumatizes us forward with an expansive resonant experience. Building coherence, synchronization, and resonance together while increasing the impact of each. The Experience of Joy connects your life with purpose, love, with something bigger than your personal id/ego. The Experience of Joy makes us more powerful by association, connection, and relationship with something bigger. The Experience of Joy changes our genetic expression, and advances, epigenetically, our DNA.

Genetic Memory

Our spirit has memory that is expressed in both our genes and in our quantum field. Quantum Mechanics is complex, but there is new understanding revealed regularly, and proof of quantum entanglement, what Einstein called "spooky action at a distance", is now able to be duplicated and measured. (Castelvecchi, 2020) What happens here happens there at the same time, and they are not sure how or why. An example might be 'love at first sight.' Soul mates might be another. Quantum action between spirits (partly our heredity, our ancestry) is what happens in me, happens in you, simultaneously. There is sometimes a connection between people that is unexplainable and makes no sense.

When I graduated from high school at 17, I moved, alone and via Greyhound bus, from Syracuse to Seattle. I was staying with my brother on the floor of his studio apartment. I found a job, started working a lot, and was at my friend Tina's house for dinner one night when I met a friend of hers. We discovered we each needed our own place to stay and agreed to share an apartment right there on the spot. Two weeks later we moved in together. For a year, she and I shared a one bedroom/one bathroom apartment as friends, having met for roughly 20 minutes. When I think back to what in the world allowed us to meet and move in so suddenly, I recognize, with 20/20 hindsight, that there was a connection between her and I that was sudden, complete, transparent, and trusting. We just knew, and that was that. Something resonated in our spirit that was an instant connection.

Our genetic memory, as anyone who has lost a loved one can attest, is real. Perhaps you see something, experience something, feel something, or had the thought that you were doing something the lost loved one did, or it reminds you of them? Grieving is aching genes from the memory of an intense genetic connection. Your genes were closely connected (spooky action at a distance) and are probably still connected. The loss of a genetic connection is a quantum reduction in personal vibrational resonance. There is still one thing about our development they are not quite sure about – how do stem cells differentiate and know what cells to become? Yes, we have a DNA 'blueprint' from our parents, and many simply believe this process is simply mechanical, and much of it probably is. I think there is genetic 'spooky action at a distance' that impacts us from conception, stores memories, and acts on those memories. Remember we are what we remember we are. Our genetic DNA blueprint includes ancestral DNA, and some of who we are is genetic memory from a generation or more ago. My genes have genes of my heredity, so my heredity is part of my genes, and when a part of my ancestral foundation is lost via the death of a loved one, it is a genetic loss in my quantum field of connections. A broken connection, discordance. Not specific pain like a cut or a burn, a general body ache in my soul (memory), my gut(memory), my brain(memory), and my genes(memory).

I have a great love of the forest, and rivers run through my soul. My paternal grandfather was a logger, helping to establish hard hats in logging. I did not know what he did, and it wasn't until much later in life that I learned about his love of the forest **and** the people who worked there. My forest connection is hereditary. Neither of my parents – theatre people – were forest people, as I turned out to be.

There is the intellectual memory in the mind, the soul memory in the heart, the instinctual memory in the gut, and a spirit memory in our genes.

So we have:

The Mind-Brain with memory.
The Heart-Soul with memory.
The Gut-Instinct with memory.
The Genes-Spirit with memory.

Memory is important because Joyful Experiences – remembered – will relive the Joyful Experience. The brain does not know the difference between fantasy and reality. The vivid visualization you imagine will create the same physiological responses in the body as if you were actually experiencing that same activity again, creating a coherent replay of the corporal and ethereal resonance.

"Our subconscious minds have no sense of humor, play no jokes and cannot tell the difference between reality and an imagined thought or image. What we continually think about eventually will manifest in our lives."
Sidney Madwed

Recalling a Joyful thought, love, soul, or other joyful experience, and going through the experience again in your heart and soul is an emotional intelligence talent that attracts Joy. Yes, at first it will be the joyful memory, but over time you can develop the ability to experience physiological joyful feelings at will. The importance of being able to connect with the feelings of Love, or Joy are extolled by Abraham-Hicks, Joe Dispenza, and Greg Braden, to name just a few. They all talk about a focused thought on what we want to manifest in our lives, to truly resonate with that desire, and to feel - corporally and ethereally – the future experience as if it was a current reality. The powerful resonation of your mind, soul, instinct, and spirit using your brain, heart, gut, and genes allows you to Experience Joy. Conveniently, and not so conveniently.

The 'Law of Attraction' (see Madwed quote above) states that what we focus on, and think about, and talk about, begins to manifest in our lives. The Law, the mentors and coaches, all those gurus tell us if we control what we think about, when our thoughts become intentional and consistent, we can change our reality. New developments indicate the importance of feeling, or emotions, being paired with what we think about. In *Secrets of the Lost Mode of Prayer: The Hidden Power of Beauty, Blessing, Wisdom, and Hurt* Gregg Braden tells us that "…feeling…acknowledges our ability to communicate with the intelligent force that 95% of us believe in, and participate in the outcome." (Braden, 2016)

Intentional and consistent coherent thought, combined with feelings and emotions enhance our personal power and resilience. Our physical, corporal brain, heart, gut, and genes are impacted, influenced, and changed by our non-physical, ethereal mind, soul, instinct, and spirit. The research and knowledge of what we are, and who we are, is exploding into our cultural consciousness, and pointing to a resonance of quantum possibilities; a compilation of materials vibrating in concert with each other. The incredibly interesting thing is that our reality is also a compilation of vibrating materials. When we understand and learn how to Resonate with the power we have, we can use the power of our resonance to change the vibrating materials in our reality.

This completes resonating with yourself. Making the Mind/Brain, Heart/Soul, Gut/Instinct, and Genes/Spirit connections gets you completely to a cohesive and resonant state.

Congratulations! You have Powered Up to Power Level 1.0 and are prepared to Experience Joy!

Connect with the Experience of Joy community at **www.thejoyguy.com**, share your experience!

PART 4

External Coherence

Opening

The quantum physics connection, what Einstein referred to 'spooky action at a distance,' has been established as truth, although not fully understood. It seems as if everyone is jumping on the bandwagon telling us what it is and what it means. The Zero Point Field, Gaia, Dark Matter, The Holy Spirit, The Web of Creation, The Field, a Force, a Presence – whatever you call it, science has identified the 'spooky action at a distance,' and continues to work to clarify and quantify what it actually is. What we know so far is that we swirl around in a matrix of matter and energy, and that we are impacted by the matrix while we also impact the matrix. (Shout out to The Matrix.)

"What You Know You Can't Explain, But You Feel It. You've Felt It Your Entire Life. " (Morpheus; The Matrix; 1999)

Quantum physics is the science that says we are connected, to people and things, and that everything is a bundle of energy in a vibrational state of existence. Within ourselves the resonant vibration is so jumbled and chaotic, we are discordant, literally bounced between other vibrational fields. Some people call it 'situation,' 'circumstance,' or even 'fate.' There isn't a 5-minute recipe for becoming coherent, and sometimes the little freedoms we achieve plateau us. The value of learning how to resonate, how to direct our vibrational existence, is greater resilience, health, and wellness – the power of Level 1. When we understand how to pair our vibrational resonance with externalities, To another, to a group or community, the power is limitless. There is no known end, only visions of what others have connected with and been able to achieve.

PART 4

Chapter 9

Resonate with your gameboard.

Resonate with your gameboard.

The Experience of Joy can happen indoors, outdoors, internally, externally, at home, school, work and everywhere in-between. Your environment may be the inside of your car, or a seat in a class, lecture, or seminar. It might be the park or the zoo, or just your backyard. Your environment is the gameboard we navigate in our daily lives, with all our sights and smells, touches and feels, sounds and rhythms, engagements and experiences. All the physical inputs we subject ourselves to, and the ethereal way we judge and categorize those environmental inputs, come into play. This is where we exist, bounced around other's vibrational strengths.

Your gameboard environment for Experiencing Joy is extremely varied; it can happen anywhere. I was driving for my first Experience and was at once terrified and full of Joy. My first thought was would I still be able to drive? (Yes.) I felt overwhelmingly large and ethereal, but still had this small corporal presence at the center that was aware and functioning. In another Experience of Joy, I was walking in the park, just strolling along and really resonating with where I was in the moment. The sights, the sounds, the smells, and my place – where I existed at that moment, my ability to be there. And another on a retreat where I was volunteering as the cook, something I love to do. We were in Sedona, Arizona and it was the early morning when the sun has that soft amber hue and was just coming up over the red rock desert. This time I felt the Experience coming, and I resonated in it as long as I could, ending up outside for the sunrise before going back to chopping vegetables in the gilded daze of the Experience of Joy afterglow. (This is also the Experience I remember and relive the most. It is so vivid in my memory that when I recall it the impact is intensely physiological – from just the memory. This is an element of PTSD; the trauma remembered creates a physiological reaction, a behavior.) It can truly happen anywhere, and once you have started the process; it can only grow. Learn how to Resonate with to yourself, piece by piece. Every success is a power-up. Know where you are in the moment. Practice presence. This is your gameboard, your environment. Your you.

We glide through life oblivious to the sensory overload, often defensive and shielded. Watch out! That car, the weather, the person walking towards you. That dog, that bird, the other driver, and the commute. We run, run, run, and rarely allow our senses a break. Then we replay in our minds what happened, excitedly, and exaggerated with the hype and hyperbole of a newscast. Learning to resonate with your environment may involve learning to see the squirrels without being pulled by them. Pay attention, be alert, and know that your presence is either coherent in resonance or discordant and chaotic. This is *your* gameboard as well as many others, and sometimes it's like the symphony tuning, and sometimes it's like the symphony playing.

Start by taking a moment – wherever you are, whatever you're doing, smelling, seeing, feeling. Ink it into your memory, close your eyes and breathe in slowly while thinking about all the elements of your gameboard. Practice being in the moment and expanding that connection to the present. Connect to your environment, your gameboard. You can create a moment to connect – at home, at the coffee shop, in the park. This is a personal game board power up and can frequently release emotions not felt before. Power Up to Power Level 1.1 by resonating with your environment!

Connect with the Experience of Joy community at **www.thejoyguy.com**, share your experience!

PART 4

Chapter 10

Resonate with your inputs and senses.

Resonate with to your inputs/senses.

The Experience of Joy involves many if not all of our 5 senses of sight, taste, smell, hearing, and touch. These physical senses interpret physical pleasure and physical pleasure is fleeting, and this is why we continually strive for a repeat of the physical experience, whether that's driving to see something that pleases you, doing a physical activity that pleases you, eating a favorite food, whatever. Whatever pleases us we repeat. (This is behind the management mantra of 'what gets rewarded gets repeated.' We all like to win and get a prize, so we will repeat the behavior that gets us a reward.) We buy the same fast food again with 'cash back' cards. We watch the same TV show - again. We drive the same route, go to the same store, watch the same movie, do the same physical thing that gives us physical pleasure because of the delight that physical pleasure gives us. Identify what gives you physical pleasure -vs- what really resonates with you, and Power Up by connecting to your sensory input!

Visual

Ingrid Fetell Lee has an amazing TED talk where she shows us visual and spatial joy and clearly identifies what isn't' joyful. I love Ingrid's validation of bright colors and shapes and believe that visual inputs are an important ingredient in the Experience of Joy. Shapes and colors make a difference, and I love her explanation of this visual aspect of joy. My own visual joy comes from nature, usually mountains, valleys, forests, wildlife (in the wild), rivers, streams, the ocean. I feel great power and intensity from nature, from connecting to the natural world. Sunshine also gives me joy, both from the visual of clear skies and the sensation of warmth on my skin. Watching Ingrid's talk is insightful, intelligent, and gave me clear insight. I changed my life because of what Ingrid taught me about being joyful. What we see is important.

The visual is the most easily distracted of the senses, but also the most easily closed. The constant movement of other artifacts and players in the gameboard is almost always ignorantly discordant, sometimes chaotic. My Experiences of Joy have contained elements of visual inputs that were at one point moving (driving, walking) and during another static (Sedona, AZ). Relax into what you see, and you may see more deeply. Look at the colors, shades, hues, shapes, lines. See the endless creativity, the infinite variety, and think about what you are seeing. What do you feel about what you are seeing?

Your senses are your inputs, and the only way you take in information. Take back this automatic function from the subconscious and be consciously present in your vision. See vividly and make connections.

Taste

I have never had taste involved in my Experiences of Joy, so I don't know how it may contribute to the experience. I have had very joyful experiences when eating something I love, both healthy and not so healthy foods, regardless of the other senses' involvement. I have had incredibly joyful mouthfuls, from snacks to full meals (not all one mouthful), and then there is chocolate.

Light, dark, solid, liquid, plain, mixed, hot, cold, round, rectangular, cake, cookie, cupcake, brownie or muffin, and if you get peanut butter on it, I'm lost. Easter season is bad, Halloween, Christmas, and Tuesdays as well. I KNOW it's common, that a lot of people – including me - go weak in the knees at the sight, smell, or taste of chocolate, and that I am just another chocoholic.

Recently I enjoyed King Salmon with sundried tomato basil butter. The incredible juicy plumpness of the taste eclipsed physical taste and sublimely went into an ethereal ecstasy. In other words, it was good. My eyes closed and my focus shuttered to feel only the taste, texture, and smell. When my eyes opened the only thing I wanted to see was how much more I had left. Chocolate has never done for me ethereally what that fish did. I remember other dishes, too. There was a lasagna at a restaurant downtown, a steak in a chain restaurant that was so perfect I remember almost every single bite and the feeling in my body as I ate it.

Our sense of taste gives us valuable information as a physical pleasure as well as intense ethereal experiences that can be joyful. Connect to your taste, and discover how you taste, what you taste, and expand your ability to taste. This is not to become a gastronomic tasting wizard, but simply to understand the physical pleasure of taste and the joyfulness it can bring.

Smell

Aromatherapy is the use of scents to create a physiological effect. We have talked about creating physiological effects with seeing and eating, and now smelling. We use scented lotions, perfumes, colognes, soaps, candles, shampoos, and more to make us feel better through smell. Coffee, cooking, natural smells, even unconscious interactions with pheromones impact us and create physiological impacts. Lemon, garlic, wine, fresh cut grass, pizza just out of the oven, roasting meats, smoked meats – the list is long and creative. Knowing that what we smell influences our physiology I encourage you to be intentional with your scents, and when it comes to joy to be purposefully conscious of the effect and impact of aromas. Allow aromatherapy to work with your sense of smell. Essential oils are phenomenal, and we use them in our bath, our laundry, infusers/diffusers, and sometimes just crack the bottle open and inhale gently. I am instantly impacted by what I smell.

The art of smells is big business in the cologne and perfume industry, but we are not as intentional as we should be. We use sprays and spritzes to freshen our world and yet think nothing of the impact on our bodies, our minds, and our physiological state. When it comes to intentionally experiencing Joy all of our senses need to be in coherence. This includes smell. It's easy to imagine discordant sounds when listening to music, let's not dwell on discordant smells wafting through our nostrils. We change the song and plug our noses. What we smell has direct influence on our sensual and sexual interests and admirations. Smellivision TV is something they've tried to come up with. Scents are big in life and contribute to a lot of relationships and coherence. Science has also shown that we might actually react quicker to smell than to vision or hearing. Be cognizant of your smell and use it to your advantage. I have had neutral and active scents in my Experiences of Joy, but no discordant (odiferous) inputs.

Hearing

We're talking about external inputs to our senses. An important one is hearing, and what we listen to. When it comes to experiencing joy there is a concert that occurs between all our senses, a resonance when they synchronize. Hearing is a difficult one as we don't really have the opportunity to segregate what we are hearing – there is just too much noise going on around us. Traffic, the kids, someone else's music being used for physical stimulation, sirens, the TV – there is a long list of what creates a cacophony of listening disruptions. Experiencing joy does not have to be a quiet experience, but hearing needs to add to the symphony, the chorus, the song of you. Remember that joy is a resonant experience of multiple sensations, and what you are hearing is important. Taking hearing into conscious control requires listening. Performers report Experiences of Joy frequently, some describing being "lost," where time and space dissolve in concert, together with what's being seen, heard, and felt. Listen to how Steve Hampton described one of his experiences:

> "Especially when they threw it to me to lead, and I just like, I did stuff on the guitar that I've never done before. I was in such bliss and such joy that my fingers expressed themselves with that joy, like they were dancing in celebration, and I kept thinking almost as if having an out of body experience that I was Experiencing Joy for the first time in 21 years because it was just - Joyful."

An observer who saw that performance commented, "… you got lost in the moment, but the moment lasted for like 3 1/2 hours." Joy distorts time and space, and what we hear is important. Discordant sounds will create dissonance by preventing the synchronization of the body. You might get parts of it, but not all of it, like a step forward and a step backward. Imagine a beautifully played song but one instrument keeps missing the beat, or the note, or is simply out of tune. Discordance destroys synchronization. I recently started listening to classical music, and not listening to anything when I am out in nature. For me, however, music has been involved in 3 out of my 4 recent Experiences of Joy. Classical on 2, and Steve on 1. Our inputs are pathways to joy, and hearing is one that is easily cacophonous and also easily coherent. The discordance is every moment not under conscious direction, or coherent acceptance. The coherent is when you are purposeful in your auditory input, when the subconscious cacophony is turned off and you consciously choose what to listen to. Bring your hearing under conscious control and discover how what you hear creates a physiological response. Filter.

As we learn to connect to our senses, we are learning how to take a bigger conscious control of what we operate in our bodies. We start out somewhere around 5% conscious and 95% subconscious. We do not want or need complete control. We do want the increased power of being in conscious control of our inputs, our senses, to be able to create resonance, coherence.

Touch

Physical touch. YES! This is one of mine, and many others', Love Language. (Chapman, 2001) Touch is an incredible sensation that can be more intense on parts of the body than on the body as a whole. Remember as a kid the single finger touch of an antagonist and how intense the reaction was? Ever done a Polar Plunge? I am referring to the physical feeling anywhere on or in the body. Hugs are on another level, and recent research tells us hugs are much more than we thought. (Heart field, neural network) Hugs are not just an uplifting feel good gesture. Hugs connect us to the person we are hugging, and yes, even to the tree being hugged, or the plant. (I actually just recently saw this demonstrated, where a monitoring device was connected to a plant and a plant lover - who was already holding the plant and generating a response – hugged the plant and the plant's monitored response increased.) Remember your hearts electromagnetic field? Massage, chiropractic, hot showers, warm baths (with salts or oils), sunshine, intimacy – the expectation of intimacy, the physical buzz of a good workout, runners high, the list is incredible just to think about. One experience I have learned to enjoy is feeling the wind. Wind varies, from the gentle warm tropical breeze to destructive hurricane force destruction. I have learned to recognize the wind for what it is, and appreciate what it does, not what it destroys, but the change, the refreshment it brings. Physical touch is a sensation we can tune into or ignore, but when the Experience of Joy occurs, the physical sensation is large, overwhelming the senses, and absolutely touches you. My wife describes the physical feeling as "sudden, spontaneous, an escalation, physiological response, muscles shaking, trembling, hands are on fire, have to express it. Crazy, most extraordinary phenomena, lose track - timeless."

There is an intensity to the sense of touch that the other senses do not have. The skin is the body's largest organ and connecting to the input of the skin is an important coherence, and frequently one that is eclipsed in the Experience of Joy. In the expansive Experience of Joy there is a sense of being larger than the body, no longer contained within the confines of our skin.

Other senses.

Other senses that are hard to describe but easy to identify also contribute to joy. A sense of accomplishment, achievement, and overcoming, for example. Combinations of those, like overcoming and accomplishment, which create freedom, independence, or winning can enhance the sensation of resonance. Other positive emotions contribute as well to the resonance needed to Experience Joy, including gratitude, acceptance, peace, enlightenment, reason, courage, and love.

Love, as the others, are not spontaneous emotions. Lust is spontaneous – we see someone or something, and our want and desire can be immediate. Being angry enough to storm the US Capital, bomb the world trade centers, kneel on a man's neck, or shoot up a prayer group you were invited into, are not spontaneous 'seemed like a good idea at the time' ideas. At some point in the perpetrator's lives, they were at a less intense point along the emotional spectrum. Increasing your power to move up in the emotional spectrum requires input, effort. There is no spontaneous improvement in the universe – thermodynamics teaches us that – so while we might (now that we've had our nerd moment) be able to see that degradation along the emotional spectrum happens with little to no effort (or purposefully), improvement along the emotional spectrum takes effort. Conscious, directed, purposeful effort.

Resonate with your senses and Power Up to Power Level 1.5! This is often a moving target as we mature, as our tastes change. Refresh in the present to what inputs give you joy. Your artifacts, players, playing pieces, gameboard. You do not Experience Joy in the past or the future, only in the present.

Connect with the Experience of Joy community at **www.thejoyguy.com**, share your experience!

PART 4

Chapter 11

Resonate with your Feelings and Emotions – Reactions to External Stimuli

"Most people overestimate what they can do in one year and underestimate what they can do in ten years." Bill Gates

Learn to resonate with your feelings.

Elevate your feelings. Joy is on the emotional spectrum and vibrates at the higher end, at a higher frequency. The lower frequencies on the emotional spectrum create dissonance and can hamper joy from manifesting. We've discussed connecting to your senses; and here we'll talk a little bit about connecting to your emotions. Similar to connecting to yourself, connecting to your emotions is outside the scope of this book. However, there are a few emotional things that relate to resonance, to coherence, and therefore to the Experience of Joy.

Many of us have had a wide variety of emotional experiences in life. The good, the bad, and the ugly. (Shout out to the 1966 movie – The Good, the Bad, and the Ugly.) We are imprinted with emotional experiences throughout our life, and often have associated physical senses as triggers – something we see, smell, or even an experience of déjà vu can bring back the memory of the prior emotional experience. Sort of a Post Emotional Stress Disorder – PESD. This could be unfavorable, but we also know that it can be extremely favorable. Our ability to recall emotions we've had in the past is an important skill. It allows us to process unfavorable emotional memories and experiences, perhaps to step closer to resolution; and allows us to embellish, enhance, and elevate the favorable memories into cherished memories. Our emotional experiences are ours, and we can't erase them; we own them all. We can change them, making dimmer the bad, and brighter the good.

In my opinion, the emotional spectrum is the most complex sensory landscape. Has anyone else ever cried when they're happy, been angry with someone you love, gotten frustrated at inanimate objects? It seems as if emotions not only have specific places along the emotional spectrum but are co-mingled with each other in a tangled matrix. Recall the X-Y Axis and imagine the emotional graph as a plate of spaghetti with spectrums running in all sorts of directions, duplicated, forward, backward, up, down, 3 dimensional. Sorting out that mix is the realm of professionals, but understand that your complexity of emotions, as well as mine, are legitimate, normal, and part of being human. It all vibrates, all the time, and like tuning a guitar string by twisting a little knob, connecting to our emotions allows us to tune our own complex

Chapter 11

emotional landscape. For me it requires mindful incrementality and radical acceptance.

Mental and emotional wellness is not something normal, it's just a state of being we visit. We are all a little different and occupy a unique space along the wellness spectrum. Some may be better at crying, while others are better at laughing. Pick your emotion – there are those that are good, those that are bad, and those that are ugly. The most impactful lesson I got was learning that I am not stuck. There is a spectrum, and I move along that spectrum, intentionally and unintentionally. Grief, anger, love, Joy, sadness - the list is endless, and I've flowed through many. The only thing I've mastered is not getting comfortable where I am, because soon something careens up and suddenly, I'm twisted again. Crap. I was well, and now I'm not – I've moved along the spectrum. However, this means I do move, and knowing where I am allows me to move with intentional speed, direction, and intensity.

Good times, with good emotions in our memory, can be recalled and enhanced. So can bad memories, but this is a higher-level function that requires assistance. We can wind up enhancing bad juju in our heads, and I strongly discourage this. I advocate recalling good memories and enhancing those. Enhancing a memory is as simple as recalling the memory, and then going through all the details, the sights, sounds, smells, and emotions and then remembering, re-saving that memory, then repeat. What may not be a part of the memory, or is a faint part, make bigger and bolder. Enhance the good feeling, the good sight, the good smells. Practice this and recall many good memories– walks, parties, conversations, meals, sunsets, birthdays, births, celebrations, and more! This makes use of the plasticity of our brain. Neural Plasticity is the actual physical changing of the brain. (We change our physical brain structure subconsciously as we learn and experience. New research tells us that we can impact the neural plasticity of our brains through conscious effort. Think about it.) This is training ourselves to use our mind as powerful centers of positive processing and actually changing our brain. Remember, we're talking about the Experience of Joy, and using a game concept to get there. Whether or not you buy into the reality of it, you are still playing the game, and the results you get will be intentional or unintentional.

When it comes to playing the game, all is fair. I once learned that a negative thought is sticky, and that to clear or overcome one sticky negative it takes as many as 10 positive thoughts. I know in my life it works, and I have used affirmations, positive music, happy images, and more to help overcome unwanted thoughts, to change my mind. Pharrell Williams song Happy, Justin Timberlake's Can't Stop This Feeling, Metallica, Rush, The Symphony, Aaron Copland, quotes printed out and posted on my mirror, in my car. There are hundreds if not thousands of possibilities. When you connect to your feelings, you might as well resonate with good ones, great ones, or ones that resonate with you.

Pairing your resonance with your feelings activates attraction in the universe. Be careful what you're feeling when you wish and desire, it will manifest in your life in some way. Sometimes, incrementally, until suddenly you are an overnight success, or think differently, or feel differently.

The quote by Bill Gates is so true, but it isn't just one year and 10 years. It's one day and 21 days, it's 10 minutes and one hour, it's the single effort and the one hundredth effort. Most people are discouraged after one or two tries, but success is the culmination of many incremental efforts.

Resonate with your feeling and emotions, your reactions to external stimuli and Power Up to Power Level 1.7!

Connect with the Experience of Joy community at **www.thejoyguy.com**, share your experience!

PART 4

Chapter 12

Resonate with another, a purpose, a group, or community

Resonate with another, an intention, a purpose.

Once resonating with self, we are fully empowered to Experience Joy. Nothing else is required, but there are higher levels that can be achieved and to date we are not sure just how powerful an individual, partnership, or group can get. No limit has been reached, and no limit has been seen or identified. Other levels of depth and empowerment include connecting to another, connecting to an intention or purpose, or connecting to a group or community.

Resonating with another is a powerful power level. There are many references to the power of two over one throughout history, and the impact of a team can be legendary. Think sports dynasties, college or pro, and recall the focus on 'the team.' Understanding your already existing coherence allows you to be extremely powerful in communication and relationships, because you can enhance the depth of even simple acquaintances.

You pour into others as you meet and greet them. They pour into you as well. They may or may not be connected, resonant, and unable to consciously accept the power up from the meeting, but you can be. There is no loss on either part, it is a personal enhancement without taking, an acceptance without obligation. Take the good inputs, let the discordant fall away. You make waves wherever you go and whatever you do. Leave behind intentional ripples.

The power of intention has been documented by Lynne McTaggert, using investigative journalist skills to write the book "The Intention Experiment." (McTaggert, 2008) This is incredible knowledge and insight provided by years of experimental evidence – what you intend is impactful and influential in the Corporal and the Ethereal. This resonance of self with intention was a key factor in my Experience of Joy. I recommend reading Lynne's book to understand the intensity of the power of intention, and keep in mind the quantum entanglement of our past that has created your present. (We are what we remember.) Your present is going to be the past of your future, and what you intend for your future will be entangled with your present intention. Your future is dependent on your presence.

Connect to another, to an intention, to a purpose and Power Up to Power Level 2.0!

Chapter 12

Resonate with to a group, or two, or three.

If you have ever been part of a team that 'jelled,' or seemed to be 'firing on all cylinders', then you know the power of syncopation and group resonance. Recall the neural network. Perhaps you are in a band or have been in a band. The band experience is a great example of both coherence and discordance.

After learning what it takes to connect to another, the process of aligning with a group, or tribe, is easier to accomplish. Frequently it's difficult to know if the entire group is resonating on the same or similar or complimenting vibrations, and sometimes we join a group or get together only to find out that our wavelength is not the same as the group's. What we individually resonate with is discordant with what the group resonates with.

The power of one is compounded with the resonance with another, amplified, increased in ways not fully experienced or known yet. Think of long-term partnerships, 50-year marriages, 40 year careers. When it comes to a coherent team, or group, the power is frequently larger but shorter lived, perhaps a decade to 15 years. Sometimes just for an intense few years, like in a dance group or band. The group will have much more comings and goings, and the resonate frequency changes, incrementally, over time. Think of churches that have resonated for thousands of years.

Connect to two or three or a group and Power Up to Power Level 3.0!

Resonate with a community.

Connecting to a community is a huge benefit for everyone - the ability to align with an ideal or organized group pursuing a common objective. The agreement you have with the group's objective can be intellectual, emotional, instinctual, or hereditary, and sometimes we choose and sometimes we get chosen. Resonating with a community, a group of like-minded individuals who share a common desire, is a level-up activity.

Sometime ago I found I qualified for membership in a well-known and what I thought was an impactful organization. After a few years of membership, I just did not feel coherent with what the group was doing, and so I resigned. I was discordant with the group, even way back then I could realize it, even though I didn't know what I was experiencing.

Your community is you, and what you resonate with. Here we take a moment to emphasize getting to know yourself, and being flexible as you mature through your life, to increased self-knowledge and awareness. The ability to choose what you resonate with is totally dependent on knowing just that; what you resonate with. With some groups we are all-in, and with other groups we are on the fringes. The trick with resonating with community is balancing the connection to one group with the resonance with another group. Your resonance to your family group may impact your connection to a political group, or environmental group, for example. Your connection to political ideals may impact your participation in your church ideals. Drop the participation that is not resonating with you. Get rid of the discordance of needing to pay attention. Unplug for a moment. Perhaps it is worth being aware of but not involved with, or perhaps by becoming aware of it is something to pursue.

Does connecting to the group add to your resonance, or is there discordance? Connect with a community and become part of something larger is a Power Up to Power Level 4.0!

Connect with the Experience of Joy community at **www.thejoyguy.com**, share your experience!

PART 5

Dissonance and Discordance

Opening

Coming out is fraught. Whether you are simply trying to express yourself as an athlete, a singer, orator, academic, author, or have a lifestyle that resonates at an LBGTQX? space on the spectrum of life, coming out requires courage, perseverance and determination, and resilience. Most of all, it requires radical acceptance. The mental self-doubt can be intense, varied, boisterous, and sometimes vitriolic. Confusion, distrust, debilitating indecision and comfort in compliance all conspire to stifle, hold back, divert, distract, and delay. Squirrels! And we may not even be sure of what must come out, simply feeling discordant where we are, or what we are, and not sure where on what spectrum to resonate. Or our resonance may be tangled in someone else's resonance. Expression of self is fraught and there is no frictionless self-expression.

This is an instantly recognizable undesirable state. The conceptual realization of dissonance or discordance is anti–flow, chaotic. Your hit every red light, never find a parking space, always find the end of the line. There are so many things in our lives that create dissonance and discordance any attempt to address them all would be folly. There are long lists of things that disrupt the coherence of self, of relationships, groups, and communities. We know very well what they are, and yet rarely take necessary steps to remove them from our lives by either working to improve the resonance or by removing the discordance to allow us to become more resonant.

PART 5

Chapter 13

The Obstacles

If you skipped directly to this part of the book you have a good idea; but just being able to identify the obstacles and working to resolve them won't get you to Experience of Joy. It will only allow you to achieve the state of being joyful.

I don't want to write about the negative elements of discordance or dissonance, this book is all about the positive aspect of getting to the point where we can Experience Joy. This state of connection creates resonance, and it is in that resonance we can Experience Joy. I mentioned briefly that there are things that create discordance, which disrupt the resonance, creating dissonance. The volume of things that are discordant, and that take away from our resonance, is similar to the volume of information on Wikipedia. (Wikipedia, 2021) We are all aware of our own particulars, or at least we should be. What we don't like to eat or drink, don't like to listen to or watch, cold weather, hot weather. There may be colors, or plants, or smells that we turn away from. It's possible you've never considered the corporal and ethereal impacts of this discordance, and what it takes to get back into resonance.

For me, my mind processing data works overtime. I have billions of synapses, and sometimes I seem to try and use them all at once. My mind is always problem solving, always trying to figure out a new plan or work out the details of an existing plan and is rarely quiet. Working to quiet my mind has given me access to more coherence. I've talked about the colors in my life, and I am working to resolve other instances of discordance. For some, there is no chance to remove the discordance, and in those cases you can work to make your resonance encompass the activity that would normally be discordant. Possibly, embracing the chaos. There is a video on You Tube I referenced earlier about chaos and order that reminds me that even the best and biggest systems that resonate in sync sometimes dance independently, seemingly chaotic but simply in between (in the gap) patterns of synchronized resonance. Remember there is magic in the gaps, perhaps in the chaos. There can still be positive neural plasticity.

Your situation, or family, or job, or other circumstances may contribute to discordance in your persona, character, and attitude. There are many examples, from the emerging gender non-conforming in an uncompromising family, to a toxic negative work environment. I already mentioned traffic. The inability to leave traffic when you're in it and need to get through it is a good example of being in a situation that is discordant and being unable to do anything but embrace the chaos. Chaos does not have to be insane: it can simply be a disruptive state or situation. The symphony tuning up before a performance can seem discordant, and they are discordant as a community, as all the musicians individually tune their instruments. Then the discordance is gone when they start playing. The discordance of traffic dissolves when you leave the traffic. The key here is not to bring that discordance from the past event to disrupt the coherence of the present. This is sometimes incredibly difficult, as sometimes our situation, family, job, or other circumstances tattoo us indelibly. Sometimes, others bring discord into our lives as if they thrive on dissonance. Think politics and social issues – coherence is power, while discordance is fractured and weak. Being in a coherent group that fractures others into discordance is an actual strategy.

If you have negative brain, heart, gut, or genetic imprints in your past, you are in good company. And as we age, those negative imprints seem to accumulate. First, I lost my father, then my mother, then my brother lost his independence. Tattoo, tattoo, tattoo. I've had my share of failures and possess a lifetime membership in the tough luck club. Finances, relationships, situations, circumstances, vehicle mishaps, accidents, poor choices, bad choices. I know how to throw a pity party. Negative happens, in as many ways as you can imagine. The connections in our brain touch almost every other volume in the library, some revered and others reviled. Some of these events are monumental to me, and my thoughts and emotions about them deep and cavernous, or fractured so completely I can't count the pieces. Those volumes in my brain library have webs of connections, but they only play in my orchestra when I allow them. Sometimes they strike a chord or refrain without being called on. I understand the importance of my string quartet pity party, my wailing winds section, and the need to listen to them. When I work with those memories I work with them, to use my neural plasticity to enhance those memories so they are accurate, embellished where I want and diminished where I can. Somethings, although painful and discordant, I must remember. They are not dissonance – they are part of my coherence.

The discordance we experience is most often directly related to the inputs in our lives. The news is a big disrupter, but even the online community that watches others fails, flops, and faults works to prevent us from finding personal resonance as we laugh at others discordance. Curiosity may or may not have killed the cat, but it sure as heck disrupts coherence. Squirrels, all of it. Learning about the inputs in our lives, the adding of volumes to our library and the connections they make, allows us to make better decisions about what inputs we accept, and gives us more conscious control over our brain plasticity.

Inputs – what we watch and see, hear and listen - is what we think about. This is where we get ideas and thoughts, from our inputs. Neural plasticity states that when we obtain new information and add that volume to our library we make connections to other volumes already in our library and change our brain. Our thoughts are from our inputs, and our inputs change our brain. Once we start thinking about something we've seen or heard we may start delving into it, asking someone else about it, telling someone else about it, refining the connections in our brain. After a while we might start doing, acting, performing. We may have seen a food we like, started thinking about it, asked someone or looked it up online, and then tried cooking it. Inputs-thoughts-reviews-actions. This process, repeated, creates

Chapter 13

a habit, and our habits define our character. Your inputs can enhance your coherence, your resonance.

The extreme elite exercises exclusive habits, which can make their character a little extreme. This is what it may take to be elite, like an Olympic athlete. The rest of us do our best to run on the Pareto Principle, or 80/20 rule. We follow a regular nutrition plan with a cheat day. We make it somewhere around 80% consistent, but then for sanity, for recovery, or for just plain fun we relax our standards a bit and enjoy. Coherence is sometimes in the 80%, and sometimes in the 20%. We are not elite in our habits or otherwise, but we can exercise good habits most of the time.

It is incredibly easy to talk about negative stuff, to trade stories about what we've heard, seen, or experienced that knocked us back, out of synch, or might be a continuing discordance in our lives. Stopping this may be difficult, because a lot of it comes from friends, family, coworkers, school mates - our own social circle. They may be grooving with Jazz, while you're resonating with Country. There is not one better than the other, or negative, there is just difference. Understanding your own resonate state of coherence may help you to process the daily deluge and discard the discordance. Filtering our inputs is a key life skill, and what has helped me is remembering brain plasticity. When I focus on something I am creating brain synapses, developing brain power. It is impossible to turn off, but very possible to filter, perhaps later, when I decide how to develop my brain.

Personal resonance precedes Experiencing Joy. Learning to connect with our own existence and resonance is an intentional skill, and intentional practiced will give you more opportunities to Experience Joy. The Experience of Joy will empower you in many ways, in relationships, in social interactions, and in personal confidence. You will gain knowledge of a cosmic coherence, relationships, and experiences. The Experience of Joy is not just a happy feeling, it is a traumatic experience of positive resonance with a much bigger and ethereal personal presence. The experience enhances our id, or ego, our persona and profoundly propels us forward.

Closing

How many times today have you seen something that is supposed to improve your life? This week? This month? This year? Your lifetime? The inputs seem endless and sometimes frantic. If you watch TV you are bombarded by the psychological influences of the advertising and marketing industry who first try and convince you that you have a need, and then solve that need with their product or service. Friends, family, teachers, coaches, mentors, virtually everyone you are exposed to has advice for you. What I've told you in this book is not meant to make you better, or change you, or say that 'this is the way.' I've explained to you what happened to me and what it exposed me to. Since my Experiences 1,000 new things have been exposed to me, and guess what?

They all propose to be the way, or a method of improving capacity in my life, my health, my relationships, my knowledge, etc. Meditation, Nutrition, Exercise, Activities, Medicines, Supplements, the list goes on. I have a voracious appetite for wisdom, so I've enjoyed it, and learned many new things. The one thing that it all comes back to, however, is that I am a vibrating frequency of energy, and what matters is what resonates with me. As an energy entity I have power, just like everyone else, and this power exists on a spectrum from the very weak to the very strong. I consider myself to be more than very weak and not even close to very strong. There are people whose brains have been so changed by what they practice they are magnitudes of times normal. Others have ability and power I understand but have not one iota of capacity. Ingo Swann was one of those people, and I think he moved us forward in understanding of human connection potential. Ingo Swann was tested and confirmed to have the ability to see remotely, to be able to mentally watch what was going on in another location like it was on TV in front of him. (Wikipedia Contributers, 2021)

We all vibrate, we all resonate within, and most of the time, if not literally 100% of our conscious awareness, we are discordant. We are the balls on a string swinging randomly as we deal with the barrage of distractions (squirrels!), demands, and the onslaught of inputs that is an ordinary life. (Family, school, work, newsfeeds, mail/email, traffic, task list) Once in a while, perhaps during an intimate moment, or watching a movie, reading a book, enjoying a vacation with family or friends or both, we jive. We spontaneously recognize that something more is going on, there is a coherence, an impression, intuition, or some feeling that resonates and physiologically impacts. What I have found is that when I resonate, when I am coherent within, then I am more connected, more powerful, and flow comes naturally. You have this power, we are all made of the same stuff, the same source material.

Again, many try and sell us all sorts of implements and ingestions to get that feeling, but nothing fits the bill. When I Experienced Joy for the first time, that huge, incredible, amazing experience I recognized the connection, and it was a coherence within myself as well as to a universal force we all know exists. I knew in an instant resonate completeness that I was in an internal state of flow. All else was blocked out and the only thing that existed in that moment was the connection, the completeness. What I recognized was that the connection to myself – perhaps for the first time in my life – resonated in coherence. When I had my other experiences, it was because I was intentionally open to having them, and consciously pursued environments that resonated with me. I had powered up, and suddenly I leveled up – new tattoo, ink it in.

We are told to do this, perform that, swallow something, eat specific things, be in a certain mood, blah, blah, blah. What you do is what you do, but I will tell you this:

I have tried many things, legal and illegal, religious and non-religious, spiritual, guides, books, webinars, seminars and conferences. I have a lifetime of fits and starts, success and failure, achievement and awards. Intense emotions, heartbreaks, loss, and more. All of it, literally all of it, every instance of emotional experience can be put on one side of a scale and it would not even register in comparison to one Experience of Joy.

My existence has changed. I've leveled up. Come join me, www.thejoyguy.com.

Bibliography

7senses.org.au. (2020). *What are the 7 senses?* Retrieved from www.7senses.org.au: https://www.7senses.org.au

Alvi, F. R. (2020, July). *What-is-the-difference-between-feelings-and-emotions?* Retrieved February 2, 2021, from www.quora.com: https://www.quora.com/What-is-the-difference-between-feelings-and-emotions-1

Andrew Huberman, P. (2020). *Breathing Ecercises for Optimized Brain Performance.* Retrieved from ww.hubermanlab.com: https://www.hubermanlab.com

BlogPost. (2021). *The Difference Between Feelings and Emotions.* Retrieved from wfu.edu: https://counseling.online.wfu.edu/blog/difference-feelings-emotions/

Boren, C. (2017, November 2). *Like Saints after Katrina or Red Sox after bombing, Astros played for their devastated city.* Retrieved from www.washingtonpost.com: https://www.washingtonpost.com/news/early-lead/wp/2017/11/01/like-saints-after-katrina-or-red-sox-after-bombing-astros-are-playing-for-their-devastated-city/

Braden, G. (2016). *Secrets of the Lost Mode of Prayer: The Hidden Power of Beauty, Blessing, Wisdom, and Hurt* (2nd ed.). Hay House Inc.

Campos MD, M. (2019, October 22). *Heart rate variability: A new way to track well-being.* Retrieved April 18, 2021, from Harvard Health Publishing Harvard Health Blog: https://www.health.harvard.edu/blog/heart-rate-variability-new-way-track-well-2017112212789

Castelvecchi, D. (2020, January 16). How 'spooky' is quantum physics? The answer could be incalculable. *Nature, 577*, 461-462. doi:https://doi.org/10.1038/d41586-020-00120-6

Chapman, G. (2001). *The 5 Love Langauages.* Manjul Publishing House.

Compassion in Jesus Name. (2021). *What's the Difference Between Joy and Happiness?* Retrieved from www.compassion.com: https://www.compassion.com/sponsor_a_child/difference-between-joy-and-happiness.htm

Diamond, M. (2017). *The Energy Number Book.* London: Mrie Diamond Publishing.

High, B. (2021, February). *How do you define joy?* Retrieved from billhigh.com: https://billhigh.com/faith/how-do-you-define-joy/

Holden, R. (2021, February). *5 Qualities of Joyful People*. Retrieved from robertholden.com: https://www.robertholden.com/blog/5-qualities-joyful-people/

Hoshide, MD, MPH, R., & Jandial, MD, PhD, R. (2018, September). A Change of Mind: How Neuroscientists Performed A Memory Transplant. *Nuerosurgery, 83*(3), E110-E111. doi:10.1093/neuros/nyy301

Institute, H. (2019). *Science of the Heart* (Vol. 2). Los Angeles: HeatMath Institute.

Leary, M. (2020, July). *What is the difference between feelings and emotions?* Retrieved from www.quoro.com: https://www.quora.com/What-is-the-difference-between-feelings-and-emotions-1

Liester, M. B. (2019, October 31). Personality changes following heart transplantation: The role of cellular memory. *Medical Hypothesis, 135*. doi:https://DOI.ORG/10.1016/j.mehy.2019.109468

McCraty PhD, R. (2015). *Science of the Heart* (Vol. 2). Boulder Creek, CA: HeartMath Institute.

McTaggert, L. (2008). *The Intention Experiment*. Atria Books.

Morpheus, The Matrix (Producers), & Wachowski, L. &. (Director). (1999). *The Matrix* [Motion Picture]. Warner Brothers.

Nelson, D. (2007). *The Emotion Code.* Mesquite, Nevada: Wellness Unmasked Publishing.

Pathways.org. (2020). *Topics of Development - Sensory.* Retrieved from www.pathways.org: https://pathways.org/topics-of-development/sensory/

Piper, J. (2015, July 25). *How Do You Define Joy?* Retrieved from www.desiringgod.org: https://www.desiringgod.org/articles/how-do-you-define-joy

Psychology Today Staff. (2021). *Flow.* Retrieved from www.psychologytoday.com: https://www.psychologytoday.com/us/basics/flow

Robertson PhD, R. (2020, August 20). *The Gut-Brain Connection: How it works and The Role of Nutrition.* Retrieved Apriul 5, 2021, from www.healthline.com: https://www.healthline.com/nutrition/gut-brain-connection

Schramm, V., & Schwartz, S. (2018, June 19). Promting Vibrations and the Function of Enzymes. Emeging Theoretical and Experimental Convergence. *Biochemistry, 2,* pp. 3299-3308. Retrieved from http//www.ncbi.nl.nih.gov/pubmed/29608286

Stasha, S. (2021, February 14). *19+ Statistics and Facts About the Fitness Industry (2021).* Retrieved from www.policyadvice.

net: https://policyadvice.net/insurance/insights/fitness-industry-statistics/

Stierwalt, S. (2020, March 23). *Can Science Explain Deja Vu?* Retrieved March 11, 2021, from www.scientifiamerican.com: https://www.scientificamerican.com/article/can-science-explain-deja-vu/

The HeartMath Institute. (2021, August). *www.heartmath.org*. Retrieved from https://www.heartmath.org

Tony Robbins. (2021). *Tony Robbins*. Retrieved from www.tonyrobbins.com: https://www.tonyrobbins.com/

Vernon, J. L. (2017, May-June). *Understanding the Butterfly Effect*. Retrieved from www.americanscientist.org: https://www.americanscientist.org/article/understanding-the-butterfly-effect#

Wanucha, G. (2018, Fall). The Gut Microbiome and Brain Health. *Dimensions*, pp. 6-7.

Wellman, J. (2015, May 21). *What is the Biblical definition of joy? How does the bible define joy?* Retrieved from Patheos.com: https://www.patheos.com/blogs/christiancrier/2015/05/21/what-is-the-biblical-definition-of-joy-how-does-the-bible-define-joy/

Wikipedia. (2021, August 9). *Wikipedia:Size of Wikipedia*. Retrieved from www.en.wikipedia.org: https://en.wikipedia.org/wiki/Wikipedia:Size_of_Wikipedia

Wikipedia Contributers. (2021, September 8). Ingo Swann. *Wikipedia, The Free Encyclopedia.* Retrieved September 16, 2021, from https://en.wikipedia.org/w/index.php?title=Ingo_Swann&oldid=1043089762

Dictionary

Term	Definition as used
Abraham - Hicks	Authors, consultants, speakers, Esther and Jerry Hicks are hard to define other than they are promoters of a better life through connection.
Adrenaline	A hormone injected directly into the kidneys by the Adrenal glands. Also called Epinephrine this body produced simulated drug increases heart rate, respirations, and blood pressure.
Affirmations	Positive statements and quotes. Can be verbal, recorded, written, or symbols.
Ingrid Fetell Lee	Designer, speaker, author. Relates our mental health to our surroundings, and is the founder of "The Aesthetics of Joy" https://aestheticsofjoy.com/
Ancestry	The mother and father lineage we all have. Our lineage stretches back indefinitely, and long ago the importance of an ancestral line played a greater role in society.
Anomalous / Discordant	Does not match, out of sync, unusual, odd, distracting.
Antagonist	Adversary, enemy, obstacle, challenge, anything that hampers the process.

Aromatherapy	The use of scents for physiological responses. While many use scents for casual purposes, Aromatherapy is the intentional and purposeful us of scents for balance and healing. A coherence of smell.
Auditory	Sound, related to hearing. (As opposed to listening.)
Bajillion	A lot. "A huge, unspecified number."
Behavioral interventions	Actions taken by yourself or others to change your behavior. Diet, exercise, mindfulness, becoming more goal oriented, affirmations. Whatever you want to change or develop can be done with a coach, mentor, or independently, but what you are doing is a Behavioral Intervention.
Biochemical	Relating to the chemical processes of the body - hormones, peptides, proteins, lipids, there are thousands of chemical processes in the body.
Bit	The basic data point that has only two states, either a one or a zero, on or off.
Brain Plasticity	The ability of the brain to change it's structure in response to internal and external inputs.
Burning Man	Burning Man is a network of people inspired by the values reflected in the Ten Principles and united in the pursuit of a more creative and connected existence in the world. Throughout the year we work to build Black Rock City, home of the largest annual Burning Man gathering, and nurture the distinctive culture emerging from that experience. The hub of this global network is the 501(c)(3) non-profit Burning Man Project, headquartered in San Francisco, California.

Byte	A collection of 8 bits, commonly thought to encompass one character in computer coding.
Cacophony	Crazy mixed up sounds, unmatched, out of sync. A chorus of unrelated chatter.
Calorie Poor	My personal term for being hypoglycemic. Not having had enough calories to keep the body resonating, my engine running.
Cellular Memory	Current research around the concept of memory outside the brain. While the heart and the intestine have millions of neurons and neurotransmitters, cellular memory is still hypothetical. I am not skeptical, but only have anecdotal stories.
Cellular Respiration	This is simply the operation of the cells. All of them. Each and every cell in the body takes in substances, manufactures materials and equipment from those substances, and creates waste. All 725 trillion of them, all day every day. No wonder we need to sleep.
Chaos	Calmly, this would be referred to as randomness. Chaos can actually be quite energetic with discordance and dissonance. It is a mismatch among participating elements.
Chiropractic	Fixes the bones, and what holds them together.
Circadian Rhythm	The 24 hour sleep/wake cycle of the body, regulated by the Pineal gland. The sleep cycle looks like a sine wave (equal up and down portions), and there are regions along the axis of our sine wave (where it crosses between up and down portions) that create different states of awareness, rest, sleep, etc.

Claustrophobia	Fear of enclosed or small, tight places. I am not generally claustrophobic, but I much prefer the wide open spaces. Meadows, plains, mountains, oceans.
Cognitive	Conscious intellectual activity, purposeful thought and intention.
Coherence	Matching values, states, or qualities. Symbiotic, complementing, flowing together in a manner that adds value.
Cohort	A homogenous group. A group of students in a class, a team, a group in or within a club, a clique.
Colloquial	Casual communication, informal.
Colloquialism	The linguistic style used for casual communication. A very common style of speech normally used in conversation. Colloquialism uses a lot of interjections and other expressions. It makes use of non-specialist terms (no jargon), and has a evolving list of terms.
Co-mingled	Mixing of things that should be kept separate.
Conjecture	A guess or hypothesis based on a summary of information or sensory inputs.
Conscious	Actively aware, present, alert, mentally knowing, intentional thought, purposefully thinking.
Corporal	Part of the body, physical, material.
Dan tien	Also Dantian; Elixir Field, Sea of Qi, Energy Center. Stored Essence, or Jing, center of life-force energy.
Dark Matter	The stuff we can't see and have great difficulty identifying and measuring, but we know exists. Dark Matter is a colloquial term for the zero point field.

Déjà vu	The sense or feeling that you are re-living an experience or situation you've been in before.
Diffusers	A device used to emit the oil, aroma's, or consumable substance from essential oils (see) into another substance, usually air or water.
Digestive Tract	This refers to the entire pathway for salivating and chewing to pooping. Most often a specific reference to the process in the small intestines and colon of nutrient identification and absorption. Mining of substances for cellular respiration.
DNA	Genetic instructions for the construction, operation, growth and reproduction of all known life. Deoxyribonucleic acid (DNA) and ribonucleic acid (RNA) are nucleic acids.
Ego	Ego is a concept of self. It is referred to as one of Sigmund Freuds' 3 pillars/constructs of the psyche.
Einstein	Alfred Einstein. Scientist and discoverer of Special Relativity Theory. I admire Alfred as the first term - Special.
Electromagnetic/Electromagnetic Field	An electromagnetic field (EMF) is a field produced by electric charges. The electromagnetic field exists as a function of light (in fact, this field can be identified as light, but you may need to broaden your definition of light) and interacts with both other fields and electric currents. The quantum counterpart of an EMF is one of the four fundamental forces of nature.

Embodied Cognition	The concept of embodied cognition is that our ability to understand and experience is constrained by the construct of our existence. As physical entities we can only experience and understand the physical world and existence. Water, as an example, can only understand the world through it's existence as water. Further, we are participatory in the experience of cognition, and therefore there is more than simple observation. We experience/observe.
EMDR	Eye Movement Desensitization and Reprocessing (EMDR) is a method used to alter your physical, emotional, or psychological state in order to process memories, specifically traumatic memories.
Endocrine	The endocrine system is our hormonal system and consists of glands attached to body organs they inject chemicals into, directly infusing into them into the blood stream.
Energetic Memory	Research is incomplete. Energetic memory has been hypothesized as the place where things are temporarily stored before being committed to long term memory. A holding station after you learn something, after it fades from active cognition but before it makes it into long term storage. Science has been able to recall these memories, but they are not sure where from. (Not active or long term)
Epigenetics	The science of how your environment as well as your behaviors and perhaps even your beliefs can influence you gene expression.
Essential Oils	Purified essences of minerals, plants, flowers, and other scents.

Ethereal	Not part of the body, non-physical or having material substance.
Force, The Force	The Star Wars thematic element for a connection to the Zero Point Field (see) that provided insight and power to the Jedi Order.
Fraught	Full of. Usually something bad, challenging, unpleasant, risky, dangerous, or problematic. Frequently perceptual or imagined; dreaded.
Frequency	Vibration. The level of frequency is determined by the number of events over time, or the number of vibrations in a given amount of time. This sometimes appears as slow or fast, but it's the number of vibrations in time. If the time is one minute, and there are 60 vibrations, it may be said to be 60 hertz. If there were 120 vibrations in that minute it would be 120 hertz. Your heartbeat has a frequency, as does your breathing, and more.
Gaia	The earth as a symbiotic organism with embodied cognition and a sub-conscious equilibrial desire.
Game Theory	Strategic interaction between or among players and circumstances or situations.
Gastronomic	Gastro = Stomach, nom = law, rule, ic = pertaining to. Gastronomic is related to the rules of the stomach, which likes nutritious food and feeds our microbiome.
Gene Expression	Gene expression is the fundamental level at which the genotype gives rise to an observable trait. All steps in the gene expression process may be managed.

Genes	The blueprint for life, comprised of a blending of ancestry, or heredity. Applies to plants, animals, and humans.
Genetic	Relating to the genes or the heredity and ancestry. Think purebreds, and how that husbandry may have infiltrated perception.
Genetic Memory	Memory that exists at birth without any sensory input.
Greg Braden	American New Age author.
Gut-Brain Axis	Refers to the connection between the gut and the brain, primarily via the vagus nerve.
Hajj	One of the 5 pillars of Islam, the Hajj is the pilgrimage to Mecca in Saudi Arabia completed at least once. (There are considerations for ability and family.)
Hereditary	Genetic inheritance from our parents, grandparents, great-grandparents, and so on. Goes back in time indefinitely, to whatever beginning you believe started it all.
Holotropic Breathing	A physical practice of taking conscious control of a subconscious process to achieve an altered mental and physiological state.
Hormones	Chemical messengers in the body. (As opposed to the electrical signals of the nervous system.)
Human	You and me. The science describes the physical, while we attempt to define the non-physical and the connections between both.
Hype	Sales pitch, promotion, publicity.
Hyperbole	Exaggeration and embellishment.
Id / Ego / Super-ego	Sigmund Freuds 3 constructs of mental activity. The ID = instinct, ego = reality check, super-ego = morality.

Immune Pathways	There are two, and they both involve memory.
Inanimate	Non-living, like plastics, metals, and textiles.
Incrementality	A marketing term referring to the small influence multiple ads make before someone is 'converted' into buying. I use it in the same context of small changes that lead to a larger outcome.
Infusers	A device used to spread the essences of a physical substance into another medium. Loose leaf tea, for example.
Ingo Swann	The father of Remote Viewing. Author, psychic, artist.
Instinct	Primarily subconscious response to inputs, like your gag reflex.
Intangible	Nonphysical
Intracardiac neurological memory	A concept that the heart has memory as one of it's properties.
Intuition	The ethereal sense of knowing what's going to happen before it takes place.
Jean Anthelme Brillat-Savarin	Father of the low carb diet. (b1755 - d1826) "Cooking is one of the oldest arts and one that has rendered us the most important service in civic life."
Joe Dispenza	NYTimes bestselling author, international speaker, researcher, consultant and chiropractic physician.
Justin Timberlake	American singer, songwriter, and producer.
Law of Attraction	The concept that as an energy being, humans attract into their lives what they think about. Further research has tied feelings and emotions to desire and want to activate the universal law of attraction.

LGBTQX?	Lesbian, Gay, Bisexual, Transgender, Transsexual, 2/Two-Spirit, Queer, Questioning, Intersex, Asexual, Ally. Also Pansexual, Agender, Gender Queer, Bigender, Gender Variant, Pangender. In my opinion, this is only a smattering of points along the infinite variety on the Spectrum/Range/Continuum of sexual/gender identity, which is one point on the continuum of a persons voice/expression.
Love Languages	Gifts, Touch, Acts of Service, Words of Affirmation, and Quality Time. According to the book by Gary chapman, "The Five Love Languages," these are five ways we experience being loved. This book is a must read and learn.
Lust	A strong sexual desire or attraction.
Lynne McTaggart	Author of The Field and The Intention Experiment
Magic	Anything that actually takes place without scientific explanation, like love. Yes, a lot of what happens when two people fall in love can be explained scientifically, but they still can't explain it entirely. It's 'magic'.
Marie Diamond	Marie Diamond is a Feng Shui, Meditation, and Dowsing practitioner and teacher. Marie wrote The Energy Number Book.
Marie Kondo	www.konmarie.com Marie wrote the book The Life-Changing Magic of Tidying Up. She is the designer of the KonMarie method. Join the movement and www.konmarie.com

Massage	The physical manipulation and stimulation of muscles, tendons, and other bodily structures for therapeutic and recreational purposes.
Matrix	The foundation perception is built on. The matrix is a construct that represents the skeletal structure that supports what we believe and perceive, or perceive and believe.
Medical hypnosis	A method used by some psychotherapists to talk to the subconscious and plant thoughts or ideas to aid in healing/changing the body
Microbiome	The microscopic environment of the intestines and colon. The intestines, aka the small intestines, is where a lot of our microbiome and digestion exist, and to a lessor extent in the colon, aka the large intestine. The Microbiome refers specifically to the microbes that live in our gut and refine the fuel that powers our bodies.
Mindful	Aware of, conscious of, intentional.
Mise en place	Everything in it's place.' A method used in kitchens by chefs and cooks where they place all the items needed to make specific dishes in an arrangement that is convenient and useful to them in the preparation and cooking.
Muscle Memory	A memory where it seems as if your muscles perform certain actions by themselves, or aid in the performance of certain tasks.
Nature and Nurture	The conversation in human development of what comes from inputs as we grow up(Nurture) and what comes from what we were born with(Nature).
Neural Plasticity	The ability of the brain to change it's structure in response to internal and external inputs.

Neurotransmitters	The chemicals in the body that actually do the communicating between nerve cells. They are the electrons in the transmission wire - the nervous system in the body. The nerves are the wires, and neuro transmitters are the energy travelling along those pathways.
Neuroactive compounds	Substance(s) that impacts other neurons. There are many natural ones, but one that may be familiar is alcohol, which anyone who has ever had an alcoholic drink should know relaxes the quickness of neurotransmissions. Instant rust.
Neurons	Nerve cells.
Nootropics	Drugs. Nootropics are drugs that are intended to improve mental functioning. If there are chemicals that slow our neural activity, of course there are drugs that enhance our neural activity.
Nutrients	Substances required by the body for repair, replacement, rejuvenation, and other processes for operation of the human body.
Odiferous	Stinky, smelly, offending to the olfactory senses.
Paternal	Fatherly, on the male side of the genealogical tree.
Perpetrator	The person who committed the actions.
Pharrell Williams	Singer/songwriter/designer/rapper/entrepreneur. Probably more than that, but there is only so much time.
Phenomena	Refers to an actual, observable event or thing.
Pheromones	Body chemicals or scents animals emit that are detectable by others of the same species.

Physiological	The physical actions of the body in normal operations.
Pigpen®	Charles Shultz Peanuts® character always surrounding by a cloud that in some strips impacts other characters.
Plateau	A level landscape. Can also be used to describe reaching a level of proficiency and intentionally or not 'camping out.'
Polar Plunge	Going for a swim in the winter, specifically in a frozen or semi-frozen lake. Not for the faint of heart, mind, or body.
Poop Transfer	Medically called a Fecal Transplant this is the procedure when a Dr takes healthy fecal material(poop) from one person and puts it into the colon of someone who is ill. Results have proven to be dramatic and life changing.
Prescient	Foreknowledge, knowing in advance.
Presence, The Presence	A) Being present. B) The recognition of something or someone outside of ourselves, identified or not. A 'presence.'
Proprioception	Sense of body position and action.
Protein	A nutrient used by the body in may functions, most commonly in the formation of muscles.
PTSD	Post Traumatic Stress Disorder. Post = after the event. Traumatic = trauma is a physical, psychological, emotional or other event that deeply wounds, scars, or otherwise mangles. Stress = The current reaction to the past trauma. Disorder = Abnormal physical, psychological, emotional, or other reactions to the Stress
PubMed	A web site with peer reviewed scientific articles for research.

Quantum Entanglement	The physics concept that states we are connected - everything - on a molecular level currently proven to exist in some situations and not completely understood.
Quantum Field	Classical physics described atoms as protons, electrons, and neutrons as marbles in an orbit. New discoveries have shown the marbles are not really solid. Quantum Field Theory is an attempt to define a multiple particle system where none of the parts have definitive existence, only what is referred to as 'infinite freedom.'
Quantum Mechanics	The math that defines single particles in systems. Can be thought of as the mathematically derived proofs of the behavior of subatomic particles.
Radical Acceptance	Without doubt, complete agreement and fully embraced without condition.
Resilience	The ability to resist.
RNA	Ribonucleic Acid, the construction foreperson for building things from the DNA 'blueprint.' RNA takes the DNA info and then follows the instruction to get built whatever is needed.
Satiate	Satisfied, filled. There may be capacity for more, but the consumption desire has been met, the question has been answered, the yearning fulfilled.
Sedona, AZ	A beautiful town in northern Arizona, a little south of Flagstaff. Red Rock country.
Serotonin	The body's cocaine for the brain. 90% produced in the gut. See microbiome.
Sidney Madwed	The Poet for the Business World. A world class speaker, lyricist, author and poet.

Smellivision	The attempt to include smells in movies.
Spark's and spittle's	Distractions that have brightness and urgency.
Spectrum / Range / Continuum	The value for anything that can be very low to very high, very thin to very thick, very dim to very bright, etc.
Spiritual	Pertaining to things of the spirit. Most often used in reference to the Holy spirit of the Christian Trilogy: The Father, the Son, and The Holy Spirit.
Spontaneous	Unplanned, unanticipated, surprise.
Spooky Action at a Distance	The quantum entanglement concept that two atoms separated by distance react simultaneously to the action performed on one.
Squirrel!	A distraction, akin to the distraction of a dog by a squirrel. We can sometimes chase a squirrel - like a dog - for quite some time before getting back on track.
Staccato	Singular beats or notes separated form others.
Steve Hampton	Grandfather - 15 grandkids. Father of 3 amazing kids & their spouses. Husband. Businessman. Healer.
Stimulus response	Non-spontaneous activity in the body. An activity or action by the body or a body system in direct response to another action or activity.
Sub-Conscious	Unaware or non-conscious thought or actions.
syncopation	Beats that are not on the time signature. Syncopation might be said to be activity in the gaps.
Synchronicity	Something that is meaningfully related but does not have an actual connecting relation. Things seem to be connected but have no actual relation. Coincidence.

synchronization	This is when the part to a system are all functioning in harmony, or in the same cohesive pattern.
Talk Therapy	Psychotherapy focused on talking, allowing the therapist to understand the patient through guided conversations.
TED	Acronym for Technology, Entertainment, and Design. TED Talks is like Wikipedia in video format, where speakers, performers, artists, and more present 'ideas worth listening to.'
The Field	The title of a book by Lynne McTaggart that describes experiments into identifying an energy source or field that permeates everything.
The HeartMath Institute	The mission of the HeartMath Institute is to help people bring their physical, mental and emotional systems into balanced alignment with their heart's intuitive guidance. This unfolds the path for becoming heart-empowered individuals who choose the way of love, which they demonstrate through compassionate care for the well-being of themselves, others and Planet Earth. (www.heartmath.org)
The Holy Spirit	Part of the Christian Holy Trinity of God - The Father, The Son, and The Holy Spirit.
The Iceman	Wim Hoff is referred to as The Iceman due to his incredible feats in extreme cold. World record extreme feats.
The Intention Experiment	The title of a book by Lynne McTaggart that describes experiments in intentionally trying to influence outcomes.
The Web of Creation	All things, physical and non-physical. Corporal and ethereal, good and bad.
Thermodynamics	Thermodynamics is a branch of physics that deals with certain systems but whose 2nd law - entropy - has been observed in all systems.

Trauma	Emotional, psychological, or physical injury that is the result of personal harm that ranges from outwardly dramatic to insidiously hidden.
Tribe	A form of social organization of a group of people who share common characteristics.
Vagus Nerve	The biggest and baddest of the 12 nerves from the brain to the body. Communication pathway between the gut and the brain. Mood, digestion, immunity, and heart rate to name a few. "...the vagal tone is correlated with capacity to regulate stress responses and can be influenced by breathing..." https://www.frontiersin.org/articles/10.3389/fpsyt.2018.00044/full
Vestibular	Commonly known for inner ear functions of balance there is also a connection to visual inputs.
Vitriolic	Extremely bitter and caustic criticism.
Wizard	Common impression is of an older person with magical powers and wisdom in their employment. Frequently related to a SME = Subject Matter Expert of the highest ability.
Ying and Yang	The two parts to a whole.
Zero Point Field	Physics previously thought empty space was an 'ether;' it is known that we only know of 1% of matter and energy. The empty space - where 99% of matter and energy are thought to exist, is now considered to be a kind of ether, or zero-point field - the ground state, or base state, of matter. We know a lot about matter and energy (the staccato beat) and little about the zero-point field (the gap).

Further Readings:

Finding Joy, by Mac Anderson, 2008, SimpleTruths, LLC

How to Win Friends and Influence People, by Dale Carnegie, 1936, Simon and Schuster

The Brain - The Story of You, by David Eagleman, 2017, Vintage

The DNA Field and the Law of Resonance, by Pierre Franckh, 2009, Destiny Books

Joy is an inside job and it's free, by Amanda Gore and Lenore Lewis, 2015, Head2Heart Pty Ltd

Joy Seeker, by Shannon Kaiser, 2019, Citadel Press

Science of the Heart, by Rollin McCraty, Ph.D., 2015, HeartMath Institute

The Book of Joy, The Dalai Lama, Desmond Tutu, Douglas Abrams, 2016, Avery

The Field, by Lynne McTaggart, 2002, Harper Collins Publishers

The Power of Positive Thinking, by Norman Vincent Peale, 1952, Prentice Hall, Inc.

Super Joy, by Paul Pearsall, 1988, Doubleday

Molecules of Emotion, by Candace B Pert, Ph.D., 1997, Scribner

Vibrational State and the Energy Resonance, by Nancy Trivellato, 2017, International Academy of Consciousness

www.ingramcontent.com/pod-product-compliance
Lightning Source LLC
Chambersburg PA
CBHW020337010526
44119CB00001B/10